Jurisprudent Essays On AI And Law

Advanced Series On
Artificial Intelligence (AI)
And Law

Dr. Lance B. Eliot, MBA, PhD

 First Edition.

ISBN: 978-1-95-738605-8

DEDICATION

To my incredible daughter, Lauren, and my incredible son, Michael.

Forest fortuna adiuvat (from the Latin; good fortune favors the brave).

CONTENTS

Note: Visuals are collected together in Appendix B, rather than being interjected into the chapter contents, for ease of reading, enhanced flow, and to see the visuals altogether.

ACKNOWLEDGMENTS

I have been the beneficiary of advice and counsel by many friends, colleagues, family, investors, and many others. I want to thank everyone that has aided me throughout my career. I write from the heart and the head, having experienced first-hand what it means to have others around you that support you during the good times and the tough times.

To renowned scholar and colleague, Dr. Warren Bennis, I offer my deepest thanks and appreciation, especially for his calm and insightful wisdom and support.

To billionaire and university trustee, Mark Stevens and his generous efforts toward funding and supporting the Stevens Center for Innovation.

To Peter Drucker, William Wang, Aaron Levie, Peter Kim, Jon Kraft, Cindy Crawford, Jenny Ming, Steve Milligan, Chis Underwood, Frank Gehry, Buzz Aldrin, Steve Forbes, Bill Thompson, Dave Dillon, Alan Fuerstman, Larry Ellison, Jim Sinegal, John Sperling, Mark Stevenson, Anand Nallathambi, Thomas Barrack, Jr., and many other innovators and leaders that I have met and gained mightily from doing so.

Thanks to Ed Trainor, Kevin Anderson, James Hickey, Wendell Jones, Ken Harris, DuWayne Peterson, Mike Brown, Jim Thornton, Abhi Beniwal, Al Biland, John Nomura, Eliot Weinman, John Desmond, and many others for their unwavering support during my career.

Thanks goes to the Stanford University CodeX Center for Legal Informatics and the Stanford University Computer Science department for their generous support, and for the insightfual and inspirational discussions and feedback from my many fellow colleagues there.

And most of all thanks as always to Lauren and Michael, for their ongoing support and for having seen me writing and heard much of this material during the many months involved in writing it. To their patience and willingness to listen.

CHAPTER 1

INTRODUCTION TO AI AND LAW

This book provides a series of crucial essays encompassing the burgeoning field of AI and the law.

These essays are ostensibly standalone and do not require any prior familiarity with the AI and law topic. You are welcome to read the essays in whichever order you might prefer. The essays have been numbered and sequenced as chapters for ease of referring to the discussions and not due to any need to read one before another.

The essays provide a helpful overview and entry point into the field of AI and law. You will find the essays relatively easy to read and eschew arcane techno-terminology, aiming to layout the vital aspects in clear language and seeking to be readily grasped. The chosen topics entail the latest and hottest trends in the AI and law arena.

For those of you that are potentially interested in knowing more about AI and the law in a deeper way, you might consider my two other books on this subject:

- *"AI and Legal Reasoning Essentials"* by Dr. Lance Eliot
- *"Artificial Intelligence and LegalTech Essentials"* by Dr. Lance Eliot

Those are more akin to textbook-style orientations to the AI and the law field. Both books are available on Amazon and at major bookseller sites. The first book listed provides a comprehensive and detailed exploration of AI and law, while the second book tends to focus primarily on LegalTech and the blending of AI.

One of the most frequent questions that I get asked during my webinars, seminars, and college courses about AI and the law consists of what the phrase "AI and the law" actually refers to.

That's a fair question and deserves a useful answer. In a moment, I will borrow from my other books to provide an explanation about the meaning of "AI and the law" and then dovetail into a brief indication about each of the essays contained in this collection.

Per the essays, you'll end up seeing that there is a great deal of enthusiastic spirit for AI and the law, and likewise a sizable dollop of angst and trepidation about the intertwining of the two. In my view, whether you love it or hate it, there is no stopping the steamroller moving ahead that is going to infuse AI together with the law.

I would urge that any lawyer worth their salt ought to be learning about AI and the law. This will assuredly be especially important for those that are just now starting their legal careers, which I mention because the odds are that the convergence of AI and the law will have an especially pronounced effect throughout your lifelong legal efforts.

For those of you that might be going a more so academic route in the legal realm, rather than being a practitioner of the law per se, the beauty of AI and the law is that there is ample room for new research and a grand opportunity to make a demonstrative mark on the field.

Despite the fact that the field of AI and the law has been studied for many years, dating back to the beginning of the AI field itself, please be aware that we have only scratched the surface on this interweaving. Anyone with a desire to push the boundaries of these two realms will readily find plenty of rampways to do so.

If you are curious about the possible research avenues to pursue, make sure to take a look at my book on *AI and Legal Reasoning Essentials* since it provides a solid foundation on the research to-date and postulates what might be coming down the pike in future research activities. I bid you welcome to the field and wish you the best of luck in your endeavors.

AI And Law

In my viewpoint, Artificial Intelligence (AI) and the field of law are synergistic partners. The intertwining of AI and Law can generally be categorized into two major approaches:

- **AI as applied to Law**
- **Law as applied to AI**

Let us consider each of those two approaches.

AI As Applied To Law

AI as applied to law consists of trying to utilize AI technologies and AI techniques for the embodiment of law, potentially being able to perform legal tasks and undertake legal reasoning associated with the practice of law. Those scholars, experts, and practitioners that have this focus are using AI to aid or integrate artificial intelligence into how humans practice law, either augmenting lawyers and other legal professionals or possibly replacing them in the performance of various legal tasks.

Crafting such AI is especially hard to accomplish, problematic in many ways, and there have been and continue to emerge a myriad of attempts to achieve this difficult goal or aspiration. The rise of LegalTech and LawTech, which is modern digital technology used to support and enable lawyers, law offices, and the like throughout the practice of law are gradually and inexorably being bolstered by the addition of AI capabilities.

There are many indications already of this trend rapidly expanding in the existing and growing LegalTech and LawTech marketplace. Notably, the potent AI and LegalTech/LawTech combination has been drawing the rapt attention of Venture Capitalists (VCs). According to figures by the National Venture Capital Association (NVCA), the last several years have witnessed VC's making key investments of over one billion dollars towards law-related tech startups, many of which have some form of an AI capability involved.

Most of the AI developed so far for LegalTech and LawTech is only able to assist lawyers and legal professions in rather modest and simplistic ways. For example, AI might speed-up the search for documents during e-discovery or might enhance the preparation of a contract by identifying pertinent contractual language from a corpus of prior contracts.

Where the field of applying AI to law is seeking to head involves having AI that can perform legal minded tasks that human lawyers and other legal professionals perform. In essence, creating AI systems that can undertake legal reasoning. This is commonly referred to as AI for Legal Reasoning (AILR).

In a sense, legal reasoning goes to the core of performing legal tasks and is considered the ultimate pinnacle as it were for the efforts to try and apply AI to law. It is undoubtedly one of the most exciting areas of the AI-applied-to-law arena and one that holds both tremendous promise and perhaps some angst and possible somber qualms.

Law As Applied To AI

The other major approach that combines AI and law focuses on the law as applied AI. This is an equally crucial perspective on the AI and law topic.

Sometimes this is also referred to as the **Governance of AI**, though there are those that believe that to be a somewhat narrower perspective on the topic. In any case, the focus is primarily on the governance of AI and how our laws might need to be revised, updated, or revamped in light of AI systems.

You likely already know that AI is experiencing quite a resurgence and has become a key focus of the tech field, along with gaining attention throughout society. AI is being rapidly infused into a wide variety of industries and domain specialties, including AI in the financial sector, AI in the medical domain, and so on.

This rapid pace of AI adoption has opened the eyes of society about the benefits of AI but also has gradually brought to the forefront many of the costs or negative aspects that AI can bring forth. Some assert that our existing laws are insufficient to cope with the advances that AI is producing.

Thus, the need to closely examine our existing laws and possibly revamp them for an era and future of ubiquitous AI.

Expected Impacts

Let's consider how AI and the law can impact those in the AI field, and also contemplate how it can impact those in the field of law.

If you are an AI specialist, you should certainly be interested in the AI and law topic, either due to the possibilities of advancing AI by discovering how to leverage AI into the legal domain or due to the potential of how existing and future laws are going to impact the exploration and fielding of AI systems.

If you are a lawyer or legal specialist, you ought to be interested in the AI and law topic too, for the same reasons as the AI specialist, though perhaps with some added stake in the game.

What is the added stake?

If AI can ultimately become advanced enough to practice law, there is concern by some that it could potentially replace the need for human lawyers and other human legal-related law practitioners.

Some liken this to the famous and telling remark about commitment as exhibited via a chicken and a pig. A chicken and a pig are walking along and discussing what they might do together, and the chicken offers that perhaps they ought to open a restaurant that serves ham-n-eggs. Upon a moment of reflection, the pig speaks up and says that if they did so, the chicken would only be involved (making the eggs), while the pig would end-up being fully committed (being the bacon).

In that sense, AI specialists in this topic are involved, while legal specialists and lawyers are committed.

Meanwhile, for those of you squarely in the field of law, lest you think that AI specialists are to be spared the same fate of being overtaken by AI, you will be perhaps surprised to know that there are efforts underway to craft AI that makes AI, such as in the field of Machine Learning (ML), a specialty known as AutoML, which could potentially put human developers of AI out of a job.

What is good for the goose is good for the gander. Or, it might be that what is bad for the goose is equally bad for the gander.

About These Essays

Now that you've gotten an initial synopsis regarding the topic of AI and law, let's take a moment to briefly take a look at the essays assembled for this decisive collection.

Chapter 1 – Introduction To AI And Law

Key briefing points about this chapter:

- This book is a collection of crucial essays about AI and the law
- The essays are provided as numbered chapters (the sequence is not essential)
- AI and the law consist of two key facets
- One facet is AI as applied to the law (a mainstay of this collection)
- The other facet is applying the law to AI (i.e., governance of AI)

Chapter 2 - AI & Law: Legal Debugging

Key briefing points about this chapter:

- Gaining traction in the field of law is the notion of legal debugging
- Recall that in the programming or software coding realm there is code debugging
- This ostensibly consists of finding and removing bugs from computer programs
- Turns out that the same notion can be applied to our laws, debugging them
- AI-based legal reasoning tools can augment the legal debugging aspirations

Chapter 3 - AI & Law: Using General Adversarial Networks

Key briefing points about this chapter:

- New laws often proceed into a repeated legal gauntlet of legal bugs identification
- Such laws are picked apart by lawyers and run through our courts
- Some assert that legal debugging could ameliorate these repetitive cycles
- A novel approach for AI legal debugging uses General Adversarial Networks (GANs)
- This GAN essentially consists of two Machine Learning systems going head-to-head

Chapter 4 – AI & Law: Intelligent Agent Qualification Issues

Key briefing points about this chapter:

- Attorneys can get roiled during a trial by an unexpected turn of events
- This is part and parcel of practicing law and dealing with legal uncertainties
- Some though are suggesting that via AI in the law, no such legal surprises will arise
- Such a brazen assertion flies in the face of the AI intelligent agent "Qualification Problem"
- We trace the Qualification Problem and discuss its saliency to AI in the law

Chapter 5 - AI & Law: Cyborg Cyborgisation Personhood

Key briefing points about this chapter:

- Legal personhood for humans is a longstanding legal matter
- Due to advances in AI, legal arguments arise about granting personhood to AI
- This is usually an argument about whether AI is approaching human-quality capacities
- Missing from that debate is the existing and expanding "cyborg" and cyborgisation
- We need to include "cyborg" humans infused with automation and AI into the discourse

Chapter 6 - AI & Law: Machine Learning Overinterpretation

Key briefing points about this chapter:

- AI-based legal reasoning systems are getting a big boost from the latest AI advances
- The trending AI approaches consist of Machine Learning and Deep Learning
- These are computational pattern matching techniques and technologies
- At times, the output displayed indicates a high certainty or level of confidence
- Unfortunately, legal nonsense rather than legal logic might be at play

Chapter 7 - AI & Law: Transhumanism Personhood

Key briefing points about this chapter:

- Humans are generally considered as the core element of legal personhood
- This is a longstanding and seemingly quite rightful assumption
- Advances in AI and automation have raised questions about legal personhood
- Even more challenging is the matter of humans intertwined with automation
- Some assert that we need to put "cyborg" as the centerpiece for personhood

Chapter 8 - AI & Law: Distributed AI Personhood

Key briefing points about this chapter:

- A core element of legal personhood is that human beings have a singular mind and body
- This makes indubitable sense and remains relatively unchallenged
- Advances in AI have raised thorny questions about legal personhood
- Whether AI gets admitted into legal personhood is hotly being debated
- Fuel to that fire is the advent of Distributed AI (DAI) and macro-cognition

Chapter 9 – AI & Law: Cyborg-Led Justice To Stagnation

Key briefing points about this chapter:

- We are heading toward judicial efforts jointly undertaken by both humans and AI
- Some refer to this as cyborg-led justice or simply cyborg justice
- The hybrid human-AI judicial milieu bodes for some notable advantages
- A claimed disadvantage is that the AI will stagnate due to codification
- Another side of that coin is that the AI might be just the opposite (a bona fide evolver)

Chapter 10 - AI & Law: Thomas Jefferson Legal Insights

Key briefing points about this chapter:

- AI is slowly being infused into legal tasks and the act of lawyering
- Odds are that AI advances will increasingly gain ground throughout the legal field
- The straightforward fact is that the law and practice of law are based on cognition
- Aspirations for what AI can do is shaped notably around acts of cognition
- Words of legal wisdom by Thomas Jefferson apply to such considerations

Chapter 11 - AI & Law: AI Vulnerability To Cyber Exploitation

Key briefing points about this chapter:

- AI in the law continues to grow and mature
- There is AI being used for e-Discovery, for legal contracts analysis, etc.
- Despite the magical semblance, AI is nothing more than software and hardware
- This means that AI systems are bound to contain software bugs (naturally so)
- Worse still, those bugs might be cyber exploitable by nefarious actors

Chapter 12 - AI & Law: AI In The Law Projects Awry

Key briefing points about this chapter:

- AI in the law continues to grow and mature
- There is AI being used for e-Discovery, for legal contracts analysis, etc.
- Despite the magical semblance, AI consists of software and hardware
- Law practices need to treat AI adoption as a systems implementation project
- Cutting corners or treating the AI project without proper diligence is bad news

Chapter 13 – AI & Law: Dogfooding For AI In The Law

Key briefing points about this chapter:

- AI in the law continues to grow and mature
- There is AI being used for e-Discovery, for legal contracts analysis, etc.
- Startups are pushing forward on these AI-based LegalTech systems
- They often seek alpha and beta users by cutting deals with outside law firms
- In addition, dogfooding is a handy approach, if suitably arrangeable

Chapter 14 – AI & Law: Productizing Legal Services Via AI

Key briefing points about this chapter:

- Productization of legal services is a hot trend (aka productization of legal work)
- You take the labor of performing a legal service and shift this into a product
- Most often cited examples include TurboTax and LegalZoom
- Trying to productize is not something you ought to blindly leap into
- Handy tips and insights are provided herein, including leveraging AI aspects

Chapter 15 - AI & Law: ABA On Lawyers Knowing AI

Key briefing points about this chapter:

- AI has become an everyday topic of discussion and is pervasive in our daily lives
- The field of law and the practice of law is increasingly having AI-infused too
- It would seem that not many lawyers are yet up-to-speed about AI in the law
- Few realize too that the ABA proclaimed (kind of) a duty of competence related to AI
- Here is a look at what the ABA says about AI and what lawyers ought to be doing

Chapter 16 – AI & Law: Law Schools AI Courses

Key briefing points about this chapter:

- AI in the law is gaining speed throughout the legal profession
- One focus consists of using AI-based tools for undertaking lawyering tasks
- Another focus involves helping clients that are dealing with AI system legal issues
- Some assert that law schools need to do more toward AI in the law for their students
- A recent study of U.S. law schools examined their AI-in-the-law course offerings

Chapter 17 - AI & Law: AI Mistakes By Law Authors

Key briefing points about this chapter:

- AI in the law is gaining speed throughout the legal profession
- Articles about AI in the law are increasingly appearing and being sought
- By and large, these are usually written by legal-oriented authors
- This in turn typically reveals that the AI side of the discussions are rather weak
- Here is what to watch out for and hopefully improve in that regard

Chapter 18 - AI & Law: Artificial Complex Litigation

Key briefing points about this chapter:

- AI in the law is gaining speed and there is little doubt of a rising trajectory
- Usual ways of applying AI include e-Discovery, doing legal contracts analyses, etc.
- Another potential focus would be in aiding litigations, especially complex ones
- Recent research highlights four key roles of AI in litigation matters
- There are both merits to using AI in litigation and caveats to be noted too

Chapter 19 - AI & Law: Legal Goals And Objectives

Key briefing points about this chapter:

- AI in the law is gaining speed and increasingly being applied to many legal uses
- Usual ways of applying AI include e-Discovery, doing legal contracts analyses, etc.
- Some legal researchers mention that setting legal goals and objective is an issue
- In essence, the claim is that AI cannot set its own legal directives, unlike humans
- This is a useful argument worthy of exploring and noting counterarguments too

Chapter 20 - AI & Law: Oxford Debate On AI Versus AI

Key briefing points about this chapter:

- AI in the law is rising as an important professional realm for the legal profession
- Meanwhile, there is a parallel growth in the study of and need for AI ethics
- Oxford Union Society recently held a debate about AI ethics
- Some controversy was that the debate occurred by AI pitted against AI
- Many insights for AI-in-the-law can be gleaned from the matter

Chapter 21 - AI & Law: Routine Legal Work

Key briefing points about this chapter:

- AI in the law is gaining speed and increasingly being applied to many legal uses
- Usual ways of applying AI include e-Discovery, doing legal contracts analyses, etc.
- There are also AI-infused legal tools gradually being made available to consumers
- Most of this is typically shaped around so-called "legally routine tasks"
- This gives rise to exploring what is legally routine versus that which is non-routine

Chapter 22 – AI & Law: Bandwagon Network Effect

Key briefing points about this chapter:

- AI in the law is gaining speed and increasingly being applied to many legal uses
- Usual ways of applying AI include e-Discovery, doing legal contracts analyses, etc.
- There are also AI-infused legal tools gradually being made available to consumers
- Some claim that whoever is first will catch hold of the marketplace
- We explore whether this bandwagon network effect will arise in AI-in-the-law

Chapter 23 - AI & Law: Theory Versus Practice

Key briefing points about this chapter:

- AI in the law is gaining speed and increasingly being applied to many legal uses
- Usual ways of applying AI include e-Discovery, doing legal contracts analyses, etc.
- Some though proclaim that we are hitting a wall on progress for AI-in-the-law
- Focus instead on crafting new theories, set aside that primal urge to build
- All told, this is commonly couched as though one side or the other can only prevail

Chapter 24 - AI & Law: Law Schools Versus Computer Science

Key briefing points about this chapter:

- AI in the law is gaining speed and increasingly being applied to many legal uses
- Usual ways of applying AI include e-Discovery, doing legal contracts analyses, etc.
- There is also the application of the law to AI, aiming to regulate AI accordingly
- Academics sitting squarely in AI-in-the-law are often faced with a tough choice
- You can reside in a law school, or computer science, though not without controversy

Chapter 25 - AI & Law: Mechanization Phrasing

Key briefing points about this article:

- Earlier on, some thought the catchphrase of "mechanized lawyering" might catch on
- We used to view something being mechanized as futuristic and advanced
- No more, with instead "automation" stepping into the popularity ring
- Topping the automation moniker has become the use of AI
- AI-in-the-law is gaining speed and increasingly being applied to many legal uses

More About This Book

For anyone opting to use this book in a class or course that pertains to these topics, note that Appendix A contains suggestions about how to use the book in a classroom setting.

Furthermore, Appendix B contains a set of slides that depict many of the salient points made throughout the book.

In some of my prior books, I've interspersed the slides into the chapter contents, but feedback by readers has generally been that readers prefer to not have the textual flow become disrupted by the slides, and instead prefer to have the supplemental material assembled altogether into an appendix.

To make sure that you are aware of those added materials, you'll notice that the ending of each chapter provides a quick reminder about the visual depictions that are available in Appendix B.

And so, with this overall orientation to the nature and structure of this book in mind, please proceed to read the essays and learn about the field of AI and law. I'm truly hoping that you'll find the essays mentally engaging and stimulative to the nature of how the law is being practiced and what the future of the law might become.

Note: *For supplemental materials depicting the aspects discussed in this chapter, refer to Appendix B, which contains various augmented diagrams, charts, and additional related facets of relevance.*

CHAPTER 2

AI & LAW: LEGAL DEBUGGING

Key briefing points about this essay:

- Gaining traction in the field of law is the notion of legal debugging
- Recall that in the programming or software coding realm there is code debugging
- This ostensibly consists of finding and removing bugs from computer programs
- Turns out that the same notion can be applied to our laws, debugging them
- AI-based legal reasoning tools can augment the legal debugging aspirations

Introduction

Debugging.

The odds are that you've uttered the word debugging, at one time or another. You must have. Debugging is a ubiquitous term that is part and parcel of our daily lives.

You ostensibly remove a so-called bug or anomaly of some kind when you debug something.

This notion was popularized via the computer field and,has become a household word nowadays. I am honored to indicate that I met and knew the considered founder of the debugging watchword, Grace Hopper, a pioneer in the computer realm and revered for her many other accomplishments too.

Her story about the origins of coining the debugging moniker is decidedly the stuff of legend. In the early days of computers, the mainstay of the times consisted of mainframe-sized behemoths that had zillions of vacuum tubes inside of them. Due to the nature of vacuum tubes, there was a tremendous amount of heat given off and there was a notable need to ensure that the mainframe was properly air-cooled.

Grace Hopper was working on one of those large-scale systems and did so inside a hut type of structure that had windows opened at the top to vent out the waves of heat. One evening the mainframe came to a sudden and unexpected halt. Grace then carefully examined the mainframe hardware to ferret out why the system had stopped.

She came upon a vacuum tube that had shorted out. The effect was akin to a string of Christmas lights whereby one shorted bulb causes the whole system to conk out. What caused the vacuum tube to get shorted? There was a moth that had landed on the connecting portion and disrupted the vacuum tube (the moth had flown in via the open vents at the ceiling).

Dutifully, she removed the moth. A log was being kept about the status of the mainframe, so she wrote in the log that she had "debugged" the system by removing the offending moth. The moth that gave its existence to history was then manually taped for posterity to the log page as evidentiary proof of the matter.

That is how the watchword of debugging began its journey within the computer field and eventually become pervasive, including spreading far beyond computing and into all sorts of domains.

The funny thing is that few people today consider debugging to be focused on hardware-related activities. We all commonly assume that debugging is primarily a software-related topic. Programmers are called upon to find any bugs in their code and dutifully remove the bugs. Coding is what we usually think of when someone says that they were debugging a computer.

The Legally Relevant Debugging Perspective

There are a few key points of clarification worth noting about debugging.

Some liken a bug to be the same as a considered error, but that is not what conventional wisdom holds.

A bug is more often is aptly depicted as a somewhat neutral contrivance overall in that it can either be a detractor or detrimental to the software (our usual meaning), or it can be advantageous (i.e., a bug could turn out to be a welcomed and quite unexpected inclusion), or something relatively benign (you can leave it in, having no adverse impact and nor adding value).

In short, we don't axiomatically know whether a bug is good, bad, or indifferent. Until you've figured out what the bug consists of, you don't know how to categorize it. Surely, we would normally not want bugs to be floating around since this seems to undercut the notion of writing code with a purpose. The theory of coding with a purpose is that all of the code exists for ascertained reasons and works as so intended, nothing more and nothing less.

A bug is then something beyond that intended purpose. The danger of this anomaly is that it could end up being malicious in some fashion. As such, many software developers would insist that all bugs are essentially defects. The proper development of software should be to always produce zero defects. If that is the case, we would never need to do any debugging if so attainable.

You might be thinking that a bug that is even relatively innocuous ought to be removed.

No sense in leaving something in the code that wasn't supposed to be there. The problem with that logic is that sometimes the act of debugging can inadvertently produce other adverse consequences. Your effort of removing the spotted bug could accidentally introduce one or more new bugs or outright errors. The old line amongst seasoned programmers is that the cure of debugging might be worse than the seeming ailment of the bug per se.

Augmented AI-based debugging tools are nowadays popular amongst advanced programmers and software engineers. The idea is that rather than a human programmer trying to by-hand find and fix the bugs inside of a program, they can use an AI tool that aids in the effort. This can speed up the debugging and also add to the integrity and correctness attained.

Why all this talk about debugging?

Because there is a growing interest in something coined as *legal debugging*.

We can use the precepts of program code-related debugging to be analogously applied to the debugging of the law.

It seems obvious that there are plenty of laws that have "bugs" such as wording that is insufficiently stated and allows for wide-ranging interpretations. Many court cases including at the U.S. Supreme Court level have dealt with varying viewpoints of even the simplest of words such as "is" and conjunctions using "or" that led to disparate nationwide viewpoints regarding the meaning and demonstrative powers of a disputed law.

As stated by Stanford Professor Michael Genesereth about the advent of legal debugging: "We have judges and courts to hear specific cases, to deal with ambiguities and exceptions and to further refine laws and regulations accordingly. And we have appeals courts and in the US, a supreme court to ensure that they do it right. From a computer science point of view, the job of these judiciary bodies is to deal with ambiguities and exceptions. They are, in effect, debugging and, through the power of precedent, repairing deficiencies in the law" (as published in the *MIT Computational Law*, December 7, 2021).

A step up in the legal debugging process entails adding AI into the detective work.

Similar to how programmers use AI-based tools to aid in uncovering programming bugs, the use of AI as applied to the law can provide capabilities to hunt for legal bugs. These AI systems examine the narrative of our laws and can seek to caution where hidden bugs might seemingly reside. In addition, recommendations for debugging the potential bug can be proffered to lawmakers and lawyers tasked with trying to expunge or mitigate such bugs.

Conclusion

You can undoubtedly expect that more tools for legal debugging will arise and they will be packed with greater and greater capabilities via the infusion of AI-based legal reasoning facets.

Imagine if we had the totality of our laws completely debugged and utterly bug-free (that's quite an eye-catcher and admittedly hard to envision).

Note: *For supplemental materials depicting the aspects discussed in this chapter, refer to Appendix B, which contains various augmented diagrams, charts, and additional related facets of relevance*

CHAPTER 3
AI & LAW:
GENERAL ADVERSARIAL NETWORKS

Key briefing points about this essay:

- New laws often proceed into a repeated legal gauntlet of legal bugs identification
- Such laws are picked apart by lawyers and run through our courts
- Some assert that legal debugging could ameliorate these repetitive cycles
- A novel approach for AI legal debugging uses General Adversarial Networks (GANs)
- This GAN essentially consists of two Machine Learning systems going head-to-head

Introduction

There is arguably a somewhat virtuous or vicious cycle that permeates the law.

The legislature crafts and enacts a new law. Over time, lawyers pick apart the law and discover a variety of legal loopholes, gotchas, and other seemingly legally imbued defects in the law. A slew of court cases arises to cope with the matter.

That's one such cycle. Soon enough, the legislator passes another new law on some other topic entirely. Once again, lawyers pick it apart finding numerous legal anomalies, the courts get enmeshed into the circumstances, and the usual series of proclamations and rulings try to straighten things out.

You might construe this as a kind of modern-day *Groundhog Day* (I'm referring to the now classic and quite hilarious movie starring Bill Murray and Andie MacDowell). We repeatedly seem to suffer from a series of repeated steps entailing a new law going through a rather bruising lawyering and jurist gauntlet, and we cannot seem to break the cycle.

Some assert that *legal debugging* could help to prevent the cycle or at least shorten up the repeating legal conundrum.

As stated by Stanford Professor Michael Genesereth about the advent of legal debugging: "We have judges and courts to hear specific cases, to deal with ambiguities and exceptions and to further refine laws and regulations accordingly. And we have appeals courts and in the US, a supreme court to ensure that they do it right. From a computer science point of view, the job of these judiciary bodies is to deal with ambiguities and exceptions. They are, in effect, debugging and, through the power of precedent, repairing deficiencies in the law" (as published in the *MIT Computational Law*, December 7, 2021).

This highlights a recent trend toward augmenting the act of legal debugging by arming the legal field with AI-based legal reasoning tools to assist in the debugging and presumed bug-fixing that needs to take place.

One such advance makes use of an AI-based approach known as the General Adversarial Network (GAN) and would be considered in the sphere of Machine Learning and Deep Learning.

To clarify, Machine Learning and Deep Learning are computer-run algorithms that typically leverage the use of an artificial neural network (loosey-goosey simplistic modeling or simulation of real neural networks but tremendously simplified). In short, these approaches do computational pattern matching.

You feed data into the tool and it will try to discover patterns of presumed interest.

Okay, so in the law, one kind of pattern that occurs during the legal debugging effort consists of identifying legal loopholes, gotcha's, and the like. When a new law is devised, there are bound to be so-called bugs within it. In a sense, those bugs are sitting in plain sight, but it isn't until later scrutiny over time that cunning lawyers and the courts come to realize there are bugs buried into the law.

Envision that we want to set up an AI system that would dig for those potential bugs and alert whenever such bugs are seemingly found. How would you devise or program an AI system to do this kind of specialized task?

One approach would be to craft a Machine Learning or Deep Learning program that would computationally crunch through law and seek to detect any inherent bugs. To get this program to work sufficiently, we would want to train the artificial neural network accordingly. The idea would be to feed lots and lots of laws that have some bugs within them, point out the bugs to the program so it knows what a legal bug looks like (considered a "supervised" or "semi-supervised" approach), and the program would henceforth have the needed patterns to ferret out bugs in brand new laws.

A difficulty in doing this would be to put together a large enough corpus of laws to make this training dataset viable for use. It could take a huge amount of expensive and limited lawyer-like resources to comb through a vast set of laws and highlight the identifiable bugs. This is undoubtedly a labor-intensive and likely costly endeavor to undertake.

Employing GAN Gainfully

Instead, we will play a zero-sum game and use AI computing to aid in our quest for generating a handy automated form of legal debugging. We will pit one artificial neural network against another one, whereby there is a neural network that attempts to do legal bug detection, meanwhile, another neural network tries to do legal bug resolutions. This is overall known as a General Adversarial Network (GAN) scheme, named to reflect that two artificial adversaries are going head-to-head. They will compete with each other in a self-supervised manner.

The inspiration for this novel approach comes from something similarly done in computer science to find coding bugs in swaths of program code. For example, a recent research article entitled "Self-Supervised Bug Detection And Repair" proffers this GAN approach that they've cleverly called BUGLAB as an apt naming for their crafted system: "BUGLAB co-trains two models: (1) a detector model that learns to detect and repair bugs in code, (2) a selector model that learns to create buggy code for the detector to use as training data" (in a research article by Miltiadis Allamanis, Henry Jackson-Flux, and Marc Brockschmidt). Their focus initially is on what some coders refer to as stupid simple bugs: "Such bugs may be thought as a form of a typographical mistake or a copy-paste error, and are often relatively hard to locate by humans but obvious after the fact."

Somewhat similar work to detect and resolve legal bugs has been done in the AI and the law field.

For example, as mentioned by legal researchers Wachara Fungwacharakorn, Kanae Tsushima, and Ken Satoh: "There have been some artificial intelligence and law studies for the imperfection of statutes but usually investigate imperfection due to logical inconsistencies or logical conflicts with primary legislation" (as stated in "Resolving Counterintuitive Consequences In Law Using Legal Debugging," *Artificial Intelligence and Law,* 2021).

They further indicate that few such studies have sought to undertake a repeated cycle-like approach: "However, there have been fewer previous studies for the imperfection of statutes due to lacking essential conditions." Thus, advancing these efforts, in their latest research they use a cycle-like method: "Then, we analyze a new set of prototypical cases with judgment (including one augmented with a retrieved set of relevant facts), a culprit, and a program representing statutes to resolve a culprit by introducing a reconstructed program so that the reconstructed program is correspondent to the new set of prototypical cases with judgment."

Conclusion

As a recap, the emergence of legal debugging as a means of preventing legal bugs or finding them soonest feasible is being pursued on multiple fronts at once. An especially intriguing and possibly powerful approach includes using General Adversarial Networks that will hone an AI-based legal debugger by having it compete against a like version of itself to get increasingly proficient at finding legal bugs.

I suppose that the old sage line rings true, namely that strident competition is said to be the spice of life.

Note: *For supplemental materials depicting the aspects discussed in this chapter, refer to Appendix B, which contains various augmented diagrams, charts, and additional related facets of relevance.*

CHAPTER 4

AI & LAW: INTELLIGENT AGENT QUALIFICATION ISSUES

Key briefing points about this essay:

- Attorneys can get roiled during a trial by an unexpected turn of events
- This is part and parcel of practicing law and dealing with legal uncertainties
- Some though are suggesting that via AI in the law, no such legal surprises will arise
- Such a brazen assertion flies in the face of the AI intelligent agent "Qualification Problem"
- We trace the Qualification Problem and discuss its saliency to AI in the law

Introduction

Any seasoned practicing attorney can recount a litany of sore points and mild traumas that they have suffered during their proud record of trying cases. Even the best of lawyers have gotten unpleasantly surprised and had their legal case go astray by an out-of-left-field moment during a trial.

A courtroom and a court case can be a jungle amidst which a wide array of wildly unpredictable and formidable legal obstacles abound.

You are stridently examining a witness and the opposing attorney makes an objection. Turns out the judge not only sustains the objection but you are also taken aback when the judge sternly advises you to give up the angle you are pursuing and move onto something entirely different. This catches you quite off-guard, especially since this series of questions was a mainstay of your case and vital to your carefully devised legal strategy.

Naturally, you decide to politely attempt to get the judge to reconsider and allow you to proceed in your line of questioning, proffering that there is a solid legal basis for the direction you are headed. No dice says the judge, and once again unwaveringly and with a bit of acrid tone tells for you to move on.

It is entirely possible that you did not anticipate that the judge would wreck your otherwise well-conceived legal argument, doing so in the midst of trial and ostensibly in front of the jury and the whole world to see. Besides the abject legal embarrassment, the more critical qualm is that your side of the case is going to be legally gutted and unlikely to seemingly hold water. This ugly turn of events is unsettling, unnerving, and might very well leave your client in rather dire legal peril.

I'm sure that fellow attorneys might assert that this lawyer bungled the matter and ideally should have been better prepared for such an intervention by the judge. Lamentedly, it is always easy in hindsight to contend that a legal strategy was deficient, though in the midst of a legal battle it is oftentimes hard to have anticipated all possible legally damaging blows that might strike at your position of the case.

This is reminiscent of the famous saying by the Prussian military commander and brilliant strategist Helmuth von Moltke in the 1800s when he stated that essentially no plan survives first contact with the enemy.

Actually, I prefer the closer translation of his German words such that you might say that no plan of operations reaches with any certainty beyond its first encounter with the enemy's main force. I like this latter version since it highlights the matter more aptly as one entailing facets of certainty or uncertainty (rather than "survival" as an all-told off-or-on condition), and emphasizes that the amassed enemy or main force is the decisive backbreaking element (rather than simply encountering the enemy in even the minutest of ways).

Reapplied into the law, one might reasonably state that no predetermined legal plan or legal strategy is going to unerringly achieve checkmate during the course of a trial. There are likely going to be bumps and bruises along the thorny path of the adjudication process.

Of course, some legal snafus can be self-forced by having insufficiently crafted your legal strategy. There are legal traps and blockages that you ostensibly should have anticipated and been ready to switch legal directions as needed. Is it fair though to claim that you should have anticipated all legal avenues and all legally obvious and also nearly legally impossible possibilities?

A realistic perspective would likely concede that it is not feasible to be readied for all permutations and combinations.

AI Enters Into The Qualification Picture

I have dragged you through this discussion about legal strategies and the realities of what occurs in courtrooms to bring up the topic of AI in the law. You see, there are pundits suggesting that via the advent of AI as applied to the law, such as the use of AI-based legal reasoning systems, there will never again be any attorney (human or otherwise) caught off-guard during a trial.

The unabashed theory being proclaimed is that AI will have covered all possibilities and ascertained all ways to deal with or mitigate any legally disrupting surprises. Sorry to soberly say that this is an abundantly tall order and generally unlikely.

One basis for disbelieving in the all-knowing AI-based legal reasoning capacity is partially due to the famous or some say infamous *Qualification Problem* in AI.

This notion dates back to the early days of AI, namely the work by Stanford AI pioneer John McCarthy and as per one of his classic papers in 1977 entitled "Epistemological Problems Of Artificial Intelligence." In that paper, he identifies that devising AI that can cover all the bases of any given situation is just not tenable for complex and real-world settings. There are dynamic states that will occur: "However, it cannot always be assumed that the other components are unchanged, especially because the state can be described in a variety of coordinate systems and the meaning of changing a single coordinate depends on the coordinate system." He uses the now-dated mental puzzle encompassing a boat, some missionaries, and some cannibals to showcase that some elements (such as the status of the boat) are dynamic and not all variants can necessarily be anticipated.

McCarthy coined this as the *Qualification Problem*, and there have subsequently been ongoing and extensive efforts to resolve the vaunted and vexing qualification dilemma (it is not yet solved).

As revealingly clarified by researcher Michael Theilscher on this thorny matter: "It arises from the fact that in natural environments the successful execution of actions can never be predicted with absolute certainty. Unexpected circumstances, albeit unlikely, may at any time prevent an autonomous agent from performing the intended actions. Planning and acting under this proviso requires the agent to rigorously assume away, by default, all of the numerous possible but unlikely abnormal qualifications of his actions, lest the agent is unable to devise plans which are perfectly reasonable although they cannot guarantee success" (as indicated in the journal entitled *Artificial Intelligence*, September 2001, "The Qualification Problem: A Solution To The Problem Of Anomalous Models").

Theilscher uses an example of a potato potentially blocking the tailpipe of a car and ergo preventing the car from properly starting, illustrating that there are always going to be unexpected qualifications that arise in real-world circumstances. Some qualifications can be considered as strong and others as weak. We can also rate qualifications as ranging from completely expected to completely unexpected.

Conclusion

Returning to the AI in the law considerations of interest herein, those that make the brash presumption that AI is going to ensure that no attorney ever again gets caught unawares in a legal argument are either conceiving of a principally theoretical world or are downplaying (or ignoring) the Qualification Problem.

Though Helmuth von Moltke would have not presumably foreseen the use of AI and nor the use of AI in the law, his somewhat modernized assertion could be recast as the rather unassailable indication that no predetermined legal plan or legal strategy stands mighty in light of what transpires once a trial gets underway and the vagaries and exigencies within the courtroom arise.

Note: *For supplemental materials depicting the aspects discussed in this chapter, refer to Appendix B, which contains various augmented diagrams, charts, and additional related facets of relevance.*

CHAPTER 5

AI & LAW: CYBORG CYBORGISATION PERSONHOOD

Key briefing points about this essay:

- Legal personhood for humans is a longstanding legal matter
- Due to advances in AI, legal arguments arise about granting personhood to AI
- This is usually an argument about whether AI is approaching human-quality capacities
- Missing from that debate is the existing and expanding "cyborg" and cyborgisation
- We need to include "cyborg" humans infused with automation and AI into the discourse

Introduction

Where does legal personhood start and end?

This is an increasingly heated and sorely debated topic when it comes to the advent of AI. Some argue stridently that we need to rethink the legal definition of personhood and make room for AI systems to be included. Others vehemently contend that until there is AI that reaches sentience, which none have and we are seemingly not even close to attaining, there is little point in carrying on regarding this ostensibly purely theoretical legally mind-bending exercise.

An added twist that is oftentimes forsaken is the potentiality for cyborgs.

In other words, one means of casting this debate entails placing humans into one category and placing AI into a completely separate and distinct category. Neither the two shall meet. But this leaves begging the question about mixing together both human and AI elements, such that we could integrate into one cohesive embodiment the fused man-machine (woman-machine) that some liken to ergo being a "cyborg" type of combination.

Legal personhood gets a lot murkier when you have a perhaps obvious semblance of personhood but one that is significantly augmented or modified by having a demonstrably crucial machine-like automation on-board too. We'll get back to this slippery slope of how much human versus how much machine constitutes personhood in a moment.

Returning to the roots of the cyborg notion, it was in 1960 that authors Manfred Clynes and Nathan Kline are credited with first coining the word "cyborg" and they did so by conceiving of a self-regulating man-machine cybernetic organism: "For the exogenously extended organizational complex functioning as an integrated homeostatic system unconsciously, we propose the term Cyborg" (as stated in the September 1960 issue of *Astronautics*). At the time, they were grappling with how to enable humans to survive in outer space as part of the early days of space exploration and the hope of one day living in space and potentially reaching the moon. Their insight was that bundling together machine aspects into a human body seemed like a feasible and sensible means to spur mankind's space-going aspirations.

Though we might construe cyborgs as a sci-fi contrivance, there is a handiness of leveraging the cyborg wording toward referring to more everyday uses of tech amidst humans.

Implants such as advanced pacemakers, robotic artificial limbs, and the like could be reasonably classified as cyborg-like systems that are integrated into the human form. This has been characterized as raising legally thorny *cyborgisation* issues: "Cyborgisation will give rise to demands for new rights. People who have lost capabilities but have not yet got the relevant prostheses will seek the right to have them. Some people will demand the right not just to recover what they are missing, but also to enhance themselves. Others will demand the liberty not to have prostheses imposed on them. Enhanced humans will seek additional rights to go with the additional capabilities that they have" (Roger Clarke, "Cyborg Rights," *IEEE International Symposium on Technology and Society*, 2010, pp. 9-22).

By and large, most of the contemporary cyborg considerations are shaped around a rather apparent showing that a human is firmly the centerpiece of the cyborgisation and the machine elements are essentially appendages or otherwise relatively clearcut physically devised add-ons. In short, the human mind remains somewhat untouched in these cyborg instances and instead, the focus is on bodily functions that are being overtaken or augmented by automation.

This raises an interesting and important distinction.

As long as a human brain is still retained and the human mind is at work within it, some would argue that whatever mixture of human body and automation you might wish to undertake does nothing to alter the seeming fact that this is a person and ergo imbues legal personhood. Even if you've replaced 99% of the body with some cyborg capabilities, but still have an intact and functioning brain and mind, they would say that there is no credible way to argue against this machine infusion as not being a legally endowed person.

Change out body parts to your heart's content, goes this viewpoint, and yet if the human mind and brain are still within, you have before you a human being.

Case closed.

Cyborg Case Is Not At All Closed

At what point is personhood somehow extinguished?

Suppose that we continue to advance AI such that the human mind becomes extended by the use of AI machinery infused into the human body. This is a ratcheting up of the problem of legal personhood. If the AI is merely adding onto the thinking processes, such that we have a 100% human mind that now has an added say 10% of AI "thinking" capacity, you would still seem to be abundantly in the personhood space (a proverbial 1+1 = 2). But if the AI becomes part of the human thinking processes and we end up with the mind at say 80% and the AI at 20%, perhaps this undercuts the personhood definition (some fractional portions that add up to 1).

Some legal scholars ask whether this is akin to the famous Ship of Theseus: "A classic philosophical puzzle about identity, ancient historian Plutarch recounts the story of the famous ship of Theseus, which was displayed in Athens for many centuries. Plutarch asked, over time as the ship's planks wore down and were gradually replaced, whether the ship became a new ship by replacing all its wooden parts or did it remain the same ship?" (stated in the *Annals of Health Law*, 2012, by Linda Glenn on "Case Study: Ethical and Legal Issues in Human-Machine Mergers Or the Cyborgs Cometh").

The personhood variations could be legally classified as:

1) Human-Standalone: Human without any infused automation or machinery
2) Cyborg of Body: Human with bodily functioning automation or machinery
3) Cyborg of Mind: Human with AI infusion for "thinking" processing
4) Cyborg of Mind-Body: Human with bodily machinery and AI infusion
5) AI-Standalone: A robot in the pure sense and distinct from "human"

Conclusion

Legal arguments that entertain personhood for AI are usually couched as Human-Standalone versus AI-Standalone. That's fine as one variant to be resolved, but it is a somewhat narrow perspective. We must not neglect the Cyborg variants.

A wiser and more comprehensive case entails grappling with the entire gamut of what falls within legal personhood.

Note: *For supplemental materials depicting the aspects discussed in this chapter, refer to Appendix B, which contains various augmented diagrams, charts, and additional related facets of relevance.*

CHAPTER 6

AI & LAW:

MACHINE LEARNING OVERINTERPRETATION

Key briefing points about this essay:

- AI-based legal reasoning systems are getting a big boost from the latest AI advances
- The trending AI approaches consist of Machine Learning and Deep Learning
- These are computational pattern matching techniques and technologies
- At times, the output displayed indicates a high certainty or level of confidence
- Unfortunately, legal nonsense rather than legal logic might be at play

Introduction

Perhaps you've had an occasion to be speaking with someone about a matter of the law and at one point either or both of you exclaimed that the underlying logic makes absolutely no legal sense.

We usually expect that any serious legal matter ought to ultimately be rooted in something legally sensible. You might not necessarily agree with the legal underpinnings per se, but at least you tip your hat to the fact that a semblance of legal logic was employed. Not all legal arguments are convincing, though we would hope that a bona fide legal argument is intelligible and argumentatively solidly embodied.

I bring up this hallowed point about being legally sensible to highlight a concern that is appearing amid the avid use of Machine Learning (ML) and Deep Learning (DL) for crafting AI-based legal reasoning systems. The overarching idea behind the use of ML and DL in the law consists of using computational pattern matching to identify and home in on patterns of legal logic.

Here's the deal in a nutshell.

You collect together gobs of legal cases. Those cases are somewhat converted or transformed into a more machine-readable format. They are then fed into a preselected Machine Learning algorithm that might be utilizing Deep Learning (generally, DL is considered a subset of ML, such that Machine Learning is a broader term and meanwhile Deep Learning is considered in comparison as a particular approach fitting within the umbrella of ML and makes use of artificial neural networks or ANNs).

A computer running the ML/DL crunches through the legal cases and seeks to mathematically find patterns of both hidden and also explicit legal logic. After doing so, you then present additional legal cases that the algorithmic setup has not previously seen, and test the discovered patterns of the ML/DL to see if the AI can solve these other legal cases. Presumably and hopefully, the ML/DL will exploit the previously uncovered legal logic to legally dissect and produce a sound legal decision for these heretofore unseen cases.

High Confidence In Legal Nonsense

Most uses of Machine Learning will typically provide an indication of the certainty or uncertainty associated with the output being generated. The AI can calculate that the output was achieved via a highly conforming fit to the modeled logic and thus seems relatively certain or has a decent probability of being accurate. Of course, it is quite possible too that the effort to crunch a prior unseen legal case might lead to a low probability of accuracy as to the predicted legal ruling since the ML/DL model perchance might not be a good fit.

If the indicated output has a low certainty, we would likely be suspicious of the output and be aptly forewarned to not likely rely upon the result. But if the certainty is shown as high, you could be lulled into assuming that the predicted result is strongly modeled and thus can be believed or relied upon.

This is where we get into murky waters.

It is conceivable that the high certainty is not based on a sound semblance of legal logic under the hood. The ML/DL model might have found seemingly non-sensical mathematical patterns that appear to do a highly confident job of predicting the legal case outcomes, yet the logic is either uninterpretable by humans or if able to be interpreted has little or no sense of a strident lawyering-like legal underpinning.

In the AI field, this is a somewhat newly raised concern ostensibly known as "overinterpretation" and requires careful diligence in rooting things out when using ML/DL. Plus, the overinterpretation can be disconcertingly problematic and at times have severely dangerous implications, depending upon how the ML/Dl is being deployed.

This shortcoming is frequently encountered in AI when using ML/DL for image processing purposes. As insightfully stated by this recent AI research study: "Image classifiers are typically scored on their test set accuracy, but high accuracy can mask a subtle type of model failure. We find that high scoring convolutional neural networks (CNNs) on popular benchmarks exhibit troubling pathologies that allow them to display high accuracy even in the absence of semantically salient features" (by Brandon Carter, Siddhartha Jain, Jonas Mueller, and David Gifford, *35th Conference on Neural Information Processing Systems*, "Overinterpretation Reveals Image Classification Pathologies").

As a revealing example of how this can surprisingly arise, imagine that we set up an ML/DL to recognize roadway Stop signs.

A human would presumably recognize a Stop sign by noticing the red color, the word "Stop" prominently displayed on the sign, and observe the shape of the sign, etc. This is all logically sensible.

To train an AI system, we proceed to feed lots of Stop sign pictures into an ML/DL and then test the model to see if it could identify Stop signs in pictures it had not previously seen.

Let's assume that the ML/DL does so with a calculated high level of certainty. We would undoubtedly believe that the ML/DL is doing as humans do, namely that the algorithm landed on factors such as the red color, the shape of the sign, and so on.

The trick afoot could be that something else is triggering the detection of the Stop signs. Perhaps the initial set of Stop sign pictures had trees adjacent to the Stop signs. It could be that the ML/DL has latched mathematically onto the trees as a pattern, and not the characteristics of the Stop signs themselves.

We know that this is non-sensical since there are lots of Stop signs that are not adjacent to trees. You could readily argue that this ML/DL is extremely fragile and unable to adequately detect Stop signs. The thing is, unless you dug into the model intricacies, you might be "blissfully" unaware of the lurking danger that this ML/DL is not robust at ascertaining Stop signs. Per the AI researchers: "When a model provides a high-confidence decision without salient supporting input features, we say the classifier has overinterpreted its input, finding too much class-evidence in patterns that appear nonsensical to humans."

Conclusion

In the application of AI to the law, we similarly would want to avoid getting caught by Machine Learning efforts that seem to have high accuracy but that are doing so for the wrong reasons. Prudent strategies need to be used to ferret out overinterpretation by AI-based legal reasoning systems.

Sensible legal logic must outweigh non-sensible legal logic (well, one hopes so). The tough challenge entails surfacing the arcane mathematics and calculations of a complex and convoluted legal reasoning ML/DL into an understandable rendition of legal logic (this can be potentially sought via the use of XAI, explainable AI, as one avenue of fruitful pursuit).

The devil, as they say, often is in the legal details.

Note: *For supplemental materials depicting the aspects discussed in this chapter, refer to Appendix B, which contains various augmented diagrams, charts, and additional related facets of relevance.*

CHAPTER 7
AI & LAW: TRANSHUMANISM PERSONHOOD

Key briefing points about this essay:

- Humans are generally considered as the core element of legal personhood
- This is a longstanding and seemingly quite rightful assumption
- Advances in AI and automation have raised questions about legal personhood
- Even more challenging is the matter of humans intertwined with automation
- Some assert that we need to put "cyborg" as the centerpiece for personhood

Introduction

Get ready for a potential upending.

It is not every day that you perchance discover that a longstanding legal precept might very well be entirely upended and turned upside down. Let me share with you one such instance. You can then decide whether the topsy-turvy claim has any legally valid merit or maybe is summarily out of order.

The place to begin is by first revealing the overarching legal precept of consideration, namely in this case it is the rather weighty matter of legal personhood. Advances in technology have increasingly worn away at traditional norms of legal personhood, partially due to the tech potentially exhibiting person-like capabilities and partially due to the merging of the human form with the likes of augmented technology.

If an AI system was developed that could seemingly do what humans can do, especially when it comes to thinking and intellectual pursuits, some assert that we would need to revise our definition of legal personhood to encompass such an advancement. Thus, for those today that insist that legal personhood is only relevant for humans per se, they would be hard-pressed to not allow for a variation that would include AI of equal (or better) intelligence than humanoids.

But this is admittedly a hard leap for those that still maintain that humans are persons and that no matter what AI you devise there isn't room to squeeze a machine into the same category as persons. You are welcome to create a new category for these artificial beings, rather than trying to overlay or overuse the person's category, the legal argument so goes.

Keep personhood summarily intact with persons, while finding or defining something else as a legal bucket to toss AI systems into.

The Inseparable Intertwining Of Human And Machine

A much tougher problem comes to the fore when you realize that there could be a mixture or intertwining of humans with a machine. If the base contrivance is a human and we add some machinery such as artificial limbs and artificial intelligence, certainly this still must be within the realm of personhood.

At the core is the human, ergo personhood presumably still reigns supreme.

The legal pickle about a man-machine combination is often referred to as the legal implications of cyborgs. I realize that "cyborg" conjures imagery of futuristic robots and sci-fi fanciful notions, but in a practical manner of speaking, we can nonetheless use the word to describe a human that has been augmented with a semblance of automation (depending upon your viewpoint, this could include a pacemaker, a robotic artificial arm, etc.).

Humans that are outfitted with integrated tech that fuses silica and flesh can be labeled as cyborgs of a sort and lean into some intriguing legal quandaries: "The cyborg as a legal entity simply does not conform to the old categorizations and their concomitant dichotomous conceptual structures of allotting everything to either to the category of persons or things. It is something new—neither human nor non-human, neither a person nor a thing" (as stated by Mika Viljanen, "A Cyborg Turn In Law", German Law Journal, 2017).

In lieu of referring to cyborgs, some prefer to coin this as transhumanism: "The modern off-shoots of the drive to fuse biological substrate and technology are found in transhumanism. Transhumanism deals with human augmentation and enhancement, with a vibrant literature discussing its ethics and risks" (per Viljanen).

Believe it or not, there are those that eschew there is anything about being human that does not in one fashion or another ultimately entail augmenting your human form with some kind of tool. In short, we are all augmented by tools and therefore it might be best to agree that we are all cyborgs in that sense of the word. As articulated by Viljanen: "To be human is to exist enmeshed with and inside technology. Humans constantly use tools, other physical implements, and intellectual resources to not only augment ourselves, but to make ourselves distinctly human. Our skills and capabilities are collections of different techniques, painstakingly arranged to form a scaffolding around ourselves to allow us to be ourselves. In this sense, humans are always cyborgs."

I have now walked you logically on a step-by-step path to the upending that I earlier promised.

Perhaps our concept of legal personhood was wrong, to begin with. The precept seems to imply that the core is an unadorned human. Instead, we should have acknowledged that all humans are ostensibly "cyborgs" of which some are less so and others are more so. A human without any machinery or automation is merely a subset then of the cyborg broader umbrella.

We seemingly need to invert our comprehension and interpretation of personhood: "If we take the cyborg imagination for real, the entire agentic structure inverts, in two senses. In the cybernetic imaginary, first, the subject-object of legal interventions is not a human. It is a cybernetic organism, of which humans constitute only one 'sub-species.' Under this outlook, humans are dethroned from the apex of legal agency. The humans may still be subjects of legal interventions, but they fall under law's influence because and to the extent that they are parts or containers of information processing entities" (as pointed out by Viljanen).

You could argue that the legal field has unknowingly been anthropocentric, placing unembellished humans at the center of legal personhood.

Oops, that turns out to be a legal mistake that causes judicial confusion today and will increasingly hamper our laws and legal efforts: "Algorithmic, non-human decision-making is bound to proliferate as robots and artificial intelligence applications emerge and become more common. This change is likely to be disruptive and challenge many established patterns in regulation and legal thinking. The core factor in the process is that advances in artificial intelligence, machine learning, and robotics will inevitably render humans increasingly irrelevant as instigators of causal chains. As a result, the law's incessant anthropocentricity will become an anachronistic burden" (as warned by Viljanen).

Conclusion

The surprising or perhaps shocking upending is that rather than bickering over what the existing definitions of legal personhood encompass, we should blast to smithereens the prevailing human centering and instead put cyborgs at the primary core. Doing so would allow for much easier parsimony in personhood pertinent legal discussions, regulatory stipulations, and the like.

How does this claimed upending seem to you?

The question for you to mull over is whether this upending holds water or whether you believe it is a backward argument that though cleverly devised is, in the end, nothing more than legally vacuous.

Note: *For supplemental materials depicting the aspects discussed in this chapter, refer to Appendix B, which contains various augmented diagrams, charts, and additional related facets of relevance.*

CHAPTER 8
AI & LAW:
DISTRIBUTED AI PERSONHOOD

Key briefing points about this essay:

- A core element of legal personhood is that human beings have a singular mind and body
- This makes indubitable sense and remains relatively unchallenged
- Advances in AI have raised thorny questions about legal personhood
- Whether AI gets admitted into legal personhood is hotly being debated
- Fuel to that fire is the advent of Distributed AI (DAI) and macro-cognition

Introduction

Let's consider a seemingly ironclad facet about legal personhood and the human condition.

I'd like to assert that one person and their intact thinking brain would constitute one semblance of personhood. Yes, that seems like a rather straightforward tally.

When we think about the nature of legal personhood, the usual concoction consists of a human being as exhibited by their body and mind. This is ostensibly a holistic notion.

Moving on, consider something a bit more complex.

Suppose we invite two people into a room to have a weighty chat on some topic of common interest amongst them. They are diametrically opposed on the particular topic. We ask them to stand face to face and carry on a spirited but civilized debate on the topic.

Now then, simple math suggests that we have two personhoods or, if you will, two personhood instances in play. Personhood for one of the two, and another countable personhood for the second participant. I trust that there is little argument over this mundane claim.

During their engrossed discussion that the two are having, they are two separable persons and they each have their own distinct agency. I bring this up because of the following consideration. Envision that one of the persons convinces the other one to alter their thinking on the topic at hand, persuading them to switch sides and come around to the other way of thinking.

Does this somehow miraculously make them into just one combined entity?

In short, have we gone from two personhoods to only one personhood?

I seriously doubt that anybody would try to make such a brazen claim. They are still two distinguishable people. The aspect that they are now aligned on their thinking does not magically obliterate their separable sense of personhood.

Case closed.

Hold on, let's not be so quick to put this case to bed.

We can add a bit of spice to the matter and add into this concoction the advent of AI.

As you assuredly know, there has been a great deal of attention regarding recent and ongoing advances made in AI. The general aspiration of those developing AI systems is to gradually and inexorably be able to craft machines that can exhibit the equivalent of human intelligence. That being said, please realize that we are a long way away from attaining such a lofty goal. There isn't any kind of AI today that approaches anything even close to sentience and nor is there any clearcut indication we are on the path toward this.

When AI Cognition And Human Cognition Get Together

Assume for the sake of discussion herein that we push and push until AI begins to rise toward a kind of cognition that humans have. An amazing feat. On the one hand, this would seem extraordinarily exciting, but we also would likely have trepidations on that score too (i.e., all those sci-fi movies have primed us that such AI will perhaps squash us like a bug).

From a legal perspective, some are already today arguing that AI ought to be granted a legal personhood status. The most extreme view is that AI and humans should both be in the same legal personhood category and indistinguishable therein. Others argue that we should set up two kinds of legal personhood, one tailored for humans and one tailored for AI. Doubters and skeptics argue that AI does not deserve legal personhood status, regardless of how far along AI progresses and even if it reaches human cognition levels.

In any case, there is a quite common misunderstanding about how AI is likely to be crafted.

One perhaps surprising revelation is that the odds are there won't be a singular monolithic AI (not at first, certainly). Instead, the more likely scenario is that we'll have lots of AI instances.

Conceive of this in the same frame of thinking that today we have thousands if not millions of program apps available to us online, and construe that we will inevitably have similarly zillions of instances of AI "apps" per se.

This takes us to the proposition that we will find ourselves in a new milieu of macro-cognition.

No longer will advanced cognition be the sole preserve of humans, as this legal scholar posits: "Cognitive ability is no more a human prerogative, but the property of any thinking machine. Crucially, it becomes possible to think that cognition can be distributed from a single human mind to technological systems comprising of multiple, carefully coordinated cognitive sub-entities" (as noted by Mika Viljanen, "A Cyborg Turn In Law", *German Law Journal*, 2017).

In the field of AI, this is being explored within a rapidly growing subfield known as Distributed AI (DAI). The overarching notion consists of how to best interconnect multiple AI systems and get them to work in some cohesive or unitary manner. By and large, the focus to date is on AI as running in machines or computers, completely separate and apart from humans and the human form.

A futuristic perspective is that the cognition of AI and the cognition of humans would interplay with each other, integrally so. If you are comfortable with that seemingly radical idea, we are faced with an interesting puzzle of how macro-cognitions or distributed cognitions will sensibly work together. We would all become cybernetic organisms of a sort. A succinct and revealing depiction of this scenario is this: "Cognition, instead, takes place in radically distributed cognitive assemblage composed of both human and non-human material and immaterial resources" (per Viljanen).

Conclusion

Let's tie all of this to the earlier points made about legal personhood.

When two humans are in a room and one of them adopts the same thinking as another (on a given topic), we agreed that there are nonetheless still two persons and ergo two instances of personhood in the room.

Empty out the room.

If we next had one AI system placed into the room that was of human cognition capability and it dialogued with a second AI system that was also of such a caliber and convinced the other to change its thinking, how many personhoods are in that room?

Your choices are that the answer is one, or two, or many, or zero.

The crux is that legal personhood and its definition and dimensions are bound to be significantly unsettled due to whatever emerges in the fervent race toward achieving AI of human cognitive merit.

Note: *For supplemental materials depicting the aspects discussed in this chapter, refer to Appendix B, which contains various augmented diagrams, charts, and additional related facets of relevance.*

CHAPTER 9
AI & LAW:
CYBORG-LED JUSTICE TO STAGNATION

Key briefing points about this essay:

- We are heading toward judicial efforts jointly undertaken by both humans and AI
- Some refer to this as cyborg-led justice or simply cyborg justice
- The hybrid human-AI judicial milieu bodes for some notable advantages
- A claimed disadvantage is that the AI will stagnate due to codification
- Another side of that coin is that the AI might be just the opposite (a bona fide evolver)

Introduction

I'm going to hit you with some hefty jargon-filled aspects and then loop around to make sure that both sides of a brewing law-in-the-future debate are sufficiently surfaced.

Are you ready?

First, there is a strident belief that we will gradually and inexorably make use of AI throughout our judicial endeavors. The odds seem to lean in the direction of at least a man-machine sharing of adjudication duties, such that AI will be employed hand-in-hand to aid lawyers, assist judges, and possibly even serve in some augmenting capacity related to jurors (a predicted thirteenth member of our juries might be a so-called robo-juror).

A further extension of the AI buttressing of human decision-making in judicial matters would be that AI does the same on a relatively standalone basis. Essentially, AI could ultimately (some assert) carry on autonomously as a lawyer, or as a judge, or as a juror (perhaps all three roles, a trifecta of sorts). Thus, rather than AI being a sidekick, AI becomes the kicker per se.

Generally, there has been a great deal of attention regarding recent and ongoing advances made in AI. The general aspiration of those developing AI systems is to gradually and inexorably be able to craft machines that can exhibit the equivalent of human intelligence. That being said, please realize that we are a long way away from attaining such a lofty goal. There isn't any kind of AI today that approaches anything even close to sentience and nor is there any clearcut indication we are on the path toward this.

The Appearance Of Cyborg-Led Justice

A sometimes used catchphrase is that we will reach a point of *cyborg-led justice*, meaning that a combination of human and AI efforts will be the day-to-day comport of adjudication.

I am somewhat reluctant to use such phrasing since the word "cyborg" is customarily reserved for a merging of the human form intimately with technology in an abundantly integral manner (think of cybernetic organisms as the defining nomenclature). A human implanted with a computerized device is closer to a cyborg notion, while a human that merely accesses an AI-infused computer system via a keyboard or by the use of a voice command is not quite in the spirit of the cyborg realm.

The more reasonably sounding phrase of a *hybrid human-AI judicial* mode of activity seems fairer as a descriptor than does cyborg-led justice.

As a side note, the variant phrasing of dropping the word "led" and simply proclaiming "cyborg justice" seems even worse to me (there are many now using that variant phrasing). I dare suggest that most would assume that *cyborg justice* refers to justice aimed at cyborgs, rather than justice being overseen, led by, and ostensibly undertaken via the use of judicially bestowed cyborg actors. One might be tempted to contend that a rose is sweeter when referred to by its best-sounding name.

Whether referred to via the cyborg naming or the lengthier moniker of a hybrid human-AI judicial mode, the overarching aim is to devise this: "A legal system designed to take advantage of the strengths of both human beings and algorithms to efficiently increase access to justice with a base level of consistency, while preserving the flexibility to address unusual and extenuating circumstances" (*Columbia Law Review Forum*, Rebecca Crootof, "Cyborg Justice And The Risk of Technological-Legal Lock-In, 2019).

In crafting that type of legal ecosystem, we would naturally seek to ensure at least two crucial factors are met, namely, per legal scholar Crootof: "Both legal stability and legal evolution are critical to law's legitimacy."

One qualm expressed about the cyborg-led justice approach is that perhaps only one of the two factors will be properly observed. The concern is that the AI infusion will abide by legal stability but at the same time will curtail or inhibit legal evolution. As notedly raised by Crootof: "But hybrid human-AI judicial systems risk fostering stability at the expense of evolution."

Why so?

The argument for the stunting of legal evolution is laid at the feet of AI codification as a cementing kind of artifact about our laws: "Translating rules and decision-making procedures into algorithms grants them a new kind of permanency, which creates an additional barrier to legal evolution. By augmenting the common law's extant conservative bent, hybrid human-AI judicial systems risk fostering legal stagnation and an attendant loss of judicial legitimacy" (per Crootof).

You see, we are presumably better off with human judges that purportedly are more flexible in their legal mulling and less prone to legal stagnation: "Human judges are sensitive to context, both to extenuating circumstances in individual cases and shifts in social norms over time, and can flexibly apply legal rules" (as mentioned by Crootof).

Let's unpack the hybrid human-AI judicial milieu and take a closer look especially at the AI element.

The prevailing contention seems to be that the AI element will by its very nature be irrefutably stodgy, serving as a stagnating imposer. In some sense, this appears to be a false strawman and a misjudged one-sided view of what AI in the law might become.

The other side of this two-sided coin needs to be given its due attention and suitably measured weight as well.

For example, if we use TurboTax as a simple stand-in for a kind of law-oriented embodiment of legal rules, you would seem hard-pressed to assert that TurboTax from year-to-year is stagnating and stubbornly clings to older age tax laws. Instead, the software is actively kept up-to-date and oftentimes even sits at the leading edge of changes in our tax laws.

This is likely more typical of what AI will bring to the legal field unless you assume that the AI will be left to languish and remain unmaintained and allowed to fall behind (I generally doubt this, in the same manner, that I doubt that TurboTax would conventionally be allowed to stagnate).

Furthermore, the contention that human judges are more apt to be legal evolvers is a rather sweeping and overgenerous embellishment. Returning to TurboTax as an exemplar, you can readily find human tax experts that are out-of-date and behind the times in comparison to TurboTax's latest updates. In a similar manner, you can readily encounter judges that retain now outdated interpretations of the laws and cling to since overturned or readapted judicial precedents.

I trust that the other side of the coin is now more visibly apparent.

Conclusion

Do not though mistake this emphasis on the potential advantages of using AI in a judicial capacity as arguing that AI will always or somehow ostensibly be preferred over humans, and nor does the hybrid of AI and human in the judicial combination necessarily strike gold.

The crux is that there are tradeoffs involved. A technological-legal lock-in via AI could indeed arise, no doubt about that. On the other hand, there is no assured lock-in that the lock-in will in fact occur. There are mitigating factors that can aid the technological-legal concoction of AI to be a high evolver and avert being a sour and inept stagnating influence.

Hybrid human-AI judicial efforts will be what we make of it. There are many possible paths, of which some are rather glum while others are more upbeat and endearing.

Note: *For supplemental materials depicting the aspects discussed in this chapter, refer to Appendix B, which contains various augmented diagrams, charts, and additional related facets of relevance.*

CHAPTER 10
AI & LAW:
THOMAS JEFFERSON LEGAL INSIGHTS

Key briefing points about this essay:

- AI is slowly being infused into legal tasks and the act of lawyering
- Odds are that AI advances will increasingly gain ground throughout the legal field
- The straightforward fact is that the law and practice of law are based on cognition
- Aspirations for what AI can do is shaped notably around acts of cognition
- Words of legal wisdom by Thomas Jefferson apply to such considerations

Introduction

I see AI in the law wherever I go.

To clarify, I see the instantiation of AI in the law for practical purposes in various realms of the legal ecosystem (sometimes on-target, sometimes a bit askew), and also simultaneously perceive the unrealized vastness of almost boundless opportunities for AI in the law.

Allow me a moment to unpack that declaration.

Initial steps today consist for example of using AI-based Natural Language Processing (NLP) to parse legal text and attempt to interpret the legal meaning and legal nuances in everyday legal contracts. AI advanced search techniques and technologies are being utilized during e-Discovery to analyze large datasets and narrow down the key portions that human attorneys ought to be closely scrutinizing.

And so on.

These though are just the baby steps toward AI in the law. As such, perhaps I should restate my opening statement and say that I see AI in the law as proffering abundant possibilities wherever I go. Those possibilities are sometimes within reach, while other prospects are quite further down the road and we will need some extraordinarily radical progress in AI to get there.

As you assuredly know, there has been a great deal of attention regarding recent and ongoing advances made in AI. The general aspiration of those developing AI systems is to gradually and inexorably be able to craft machines that can exhibit the equivalent of human intelligence. That being said, please realize that we are a long way away from attaining such a lofty goal. There isn't any kind of AI today that approaches anything even close to sentience and nor is there any clearcut indication we are on the path toward this.

When Cognition Is King

If you are wondering how you too can copiously perceive the opportunities for AI in the law, a rather straightforward way entails putting on a visionary set of glasses akin to wearing a specially devised Augmented Reality (AR) headset. This specially devised pair of glasses needs to be tuned to the particular wavelength of sensing our use of *cognition*.

That seems curiously enigmatic, so let's bring it back down to earth.

Even a casual look at adjudication reveals that the work of lawyers and jurists is principally one of cognition. You read up on the law and cognitively think about what it portends. You craft legal arguments based on your cognitive skills. You spar with opposing attorneys in a cognitive-laden milieu to see which is better able to think about the law and compose the strongest legal arguments. Etc.

The bulk of the lawyering task has to do with cognition, while physicality is merely a tag-along as it were. Working in the field of law can be reasonably construed as working in a cognition dominant profession. Contrast this with other professions. A home builder presumably does a lot of physical work in constructing a home, more so than the cognitive work required (of course, designing or architecting a structure is cognitively steeped).

I bring up the vital nature of cognition as instrumental to the law and the practice of law to illuminate the golden allure of AI as applied to the law.

The emphasis on AI is to create machines or computers that can provide cognition on a level equal to (maybe eventually better than?) that of humans. When you look around and wonder where AI is going to be best applied, the easiest answer is to find settings that invoke a chockful of cognition.

Rather than consuming *human* cognition for a given task, the question will be whether AI can stand in place of human cognition instead.

I'd like to invoke a favored elucidation about the law that will aid in revealing the vitalness of cognition and the legal mind.

In a now-famous letter that Thomas Jefferson wrote, he provided these enduring words: "I am certainly not an advocate for frequent and untried changes in laws and constitutions. But I know also, that laws and institutions must go hand in hand with the progress of the human mind. As that becomes more developed, more enlightened, as new discoveries are made, new truths disclosed, and manners and opinions change with the change of circumstances, institutions must advance also, and keep pace with the times. We might as well require a man to wear still the coat which fitted him when a boy, as civilized society to remain ever under the regimen of their barbarous ancestors" (in a letter sent by Jefferson to Samuel Kercheval aka Henry Tompkinson, dated July 12, 1816).

Jefferson foresaw that the nature of law and the task of lawyering will change over time. To some degree, this change arises due to the progress and advancement of the human mind. In that same vein, the advent of AI will seemingly spur the human mind, acting either directly or indirectly as an aid to the human mind. You see, AI provides the promise of bolstering our cognition and accordingly, inevitably, dovetailing into the cognition underlying the practice of law.

Conclusion

Some wring their hands that AI might have the opposite effect of the aforementioned progression. Perhaps AI will become a solidifier that curtails or dampens changes in the law and lawyering efforts. Furthermore, the human mind might decay by an overreliance on AI. A double whammy, therefore, arises, whereby the human mind is less capable than before, plus AI itself is stuck in a programming rut and remains woefully out of date.

The law suffers, justice suffers, human lawyers are adrift.

I am doubtful of such an outcome emerging, though we must remain ever vigilant to ensure that the AI we devise does not prompt us upon such a dour path. One might optimistically ask, will our future selves that are armed with AI be looking back at the law and lawyering as it existed before AI, and wonder what kind of barbarous ancestors we once were? Or, for those of a doomsday variety, will our future selves be wishfully thinking those were the good old days (before AI became pervasive in the law)?

We get to decide, we get to pave the road ahead.

Thomas Jefferson memorably questioned how much pain has cost us the evils which have never happened. Another of his witticisms seems equally applicable, never put off till tomorrow what you can do today.

Note: *For supplemental materials depicting the aspects discussed in this chapter, refer to Appendix B, which contains various augmented diagrams, charts, and additional related facets of relevance.*

CHAPTER 11
AI & LAW:
AI VULNERABILITY TO CYBER EXPLOITATION

Key briefing points about this article:

- AI in the law continues to grow and mature
- There is AI being used for e-Discovery, for legal contracts analysis, etc.
- Despite the magical semblance, AI is nothing more than software and hardware
- This means that AI systems are bound to contain software bugs (naturally so)
- Worse still, those bugs might be cyber exploitable by nefarious actors

Introduction

AI in the law is gaining increasing traction, which also means that there are increased chances of a crushing domino effect from underlying software bugs and cyber exploitations aimed at the growing base of AI-infused jurisprudence systems.

Let's unpack that assertion.

As you assuredly know, there has been a great deal of attention regarding recent and ongoing advances made in AI in the law. Initial steps consist for example of using AI-based Natural Language Processing (NLP) to parse legal text and attempt to interpret the legal meaning and legal nuances in everyday legal contracts. AI advanced search techniques and technologies are being utilized during e-Discovery to analyze large datasets and narrow down the key portions that human attorneys ought to be closely scrutinizing.

And so on.

We can add a bit of spice to the matter and add into this concoction the advent of so-called robo-lawyers, along with the even more distantly practical robo-judges and robo-jurors (a trifecta of AI in the law, as it were). The general aspiration of those developing AI systems is to gradually and inexorably be able to craft machines that can exhibit the equivalent of human intelligence. That being said, please realize that we are a long way away from attaining such a lofty goal. There isn't any kind of AI today that approaches anything even close to sentience and nor is there any clearcut indication we are on the path toward this.

The Hard Truth About AI Vulnerabilities And Exploitability

When discussing the topic of AI, it is important to keep in mind that we are referring to nothing more than an everyday piece of software that runs on some semblance of computer hardware. I say this because the AI moniker oftentimes invokes wild notions of an otherworldly contrivance. The reality is that AI of today is merely an advanced formulation of software that either runs on conventional computer hardware or might utilize specialized hardware devised specifically for AI-based algorithms.

I bring us back down to earth about AI to emphasize that ergo the use of AI is as vulnerable to containing software bugs in the same manner that your fun app on your smartphone for tracking home cooking recipes might have embedded coding errors. Or likewise, the software on your laptop or a cloud software-as-a-service system might have a bug hidden within it. AI can readily also contain programming flaws.

You must dispense entirely from your mind that the aura of AI somehow miraculously also suggests that the AI system will be completely error-free. This is summarily and categorically a false impression.

On top of that crucial notion, there is another add-on factor about bugs that you should be mulling over carefully, namely that bugs can sometimes be exploited by nefarious actors. If a bug is discovered in a program, this opens the door to potentially exploiting the bug for insidious purposes. Of course, it all depends upon what the nature of the bug is, along with whether the software containing the bug is worthy of being attacked.

Cyber attacking a home cooking recipe program might not be worth the effort for any tried-and-true evildoer. Unless the exploitation can produce a money-making outcome or proffer other advantages, perhaps entailing stealing precious data or compromising someone such that it generates value to the cyber hacker, there is little incentive to pursue the bug.

In the field of software, we normally refer to a *software stack*, doing so to illuminate the fact that most software consists of layers upon layers of programs. Rarely is a program a singular cohesive monolith. Instead, most software uses a slew of other software components and allied programs to help out in attaining whatever the core software is supposed to accomplish. This is also known as the *software supply chain* in terms of piecing together an overall program by collecting together numerous other software components from a myriad of sources.

I have dragged you through this elucidation to land on the rising qualm that AI in the law systems are undoubtedly and inexorably going to contain bugs (they likely already do), and those bugs could be potentially cyber exploited in the worst of ways.

How bad can a bug generally be in terms of opening Pandora's box?

As an example of how far-reaching such matters can take us, consider a recent headline-stoking worldwide impacting software bug identified in an otherwise obscure open-source program known as Log4Shell that is within the Log4j software library (the bug and its exploitation are referred to collectively as *the Log4j*, and the nitty-gritty details about it can be found in the official system-security posting CVE-2021-44228).

Here's the deal.

The program is a for-free piece of code that is typically used to keep tabs on how computer servers are being used, such as logging each time a user accesses the server or each time that an app runs on a given server. Anyone setting up a server would conventionally agree that this logging program is quite handy to include. System administrators that are responsible for monitoring a server have routinely installed the logger program (either knowingly or more often somewhat unknowingly as a routine matter).

Estimates are that the Log4j logger program is installed on hundreds of thousands of servers worldwide and has been downloaded millions of times for presumed potential use and installation.

The program is especially popular because it is free to use, relatively easy to use, and provides a useful function that is assumed to be innocuous and readily employed. Also, the program is widely popular and therefore assumed to be stable and reliable. You see, since seemingly everyone else uses it, you might as well use it too (that's been the prevailing assumption, i.e. wisdom of the crowd).

Note that heretofore the world at large has not especially been aware of Log4j, as it is something that only sys admins and the like cared about (and, amongst them, Log4j was a kind of no-brainer per se).

Turns out that a lurking bug existed in Log4j, sitting there for years. The bug allows an ability to force a remote execution of code upon a server that is using Log4j. In brief, this means an unsettling and dangerous cyber exploitation exists for intruders seeking to remotely take over the server or possibly force the server to run malware, ransomware, and other infectious software devised by a cyber crook.

That's bad.

Equally painful is that the exploitation of the bug is nearly trivial to undertake. A cyber attacker can just send an email or set an account name that will trigger the bug to do what they despicably hope to do. Apparently, foul hackers discovered the bug and had been quietly exploiting it for at least several weeks before a widespread realization arose that the bug and exploit were taking place. In this so-called everywhere problem, system administrators have been putting in place an updated version or patch to the Log4j gaping hole, though you can bet that many servers will not get patched and the vulnerability will stay amongst us for years to come.

Shifting gears, the same overall type of vulnerability exists for AI systems, including AI in the law systems.

An exploitable bug might be directly within the AI system itself, or might be residing in some unobtrusive component in the overall software stack supporting the AI system. Envision that an AI system for aiding judges in their adjudication efforts was to contain such an exploit. Or, envision a law practice using AI to undertake e-Discovery or analyze contracts having an exploit buried deep within the code.

We will need to be keeping a close eye on the exploitable vulnerabilities of AI in the law systems.

Conclusion

Speaking of eyes being watchful, advocates of openness for software have all along asserted that open-source software is the safest kind of software because it is openly available and therefore is scrutinized (presumably) by thousands or maybe millions of programmers across the globe. As such, the assumption is that no bugs or exploits would exist, due to the intense scrutiny of openness versus custom or proprietary software.

The Log4j instance showcases that there is no free lunch and open-source is not a guaranteed error-free and exploit-free avenue for software.

Note: *For supplemental materials depicting the aspects discussed in this chapter, refer to Appendix B, which contains various augmented diagrams, charts, and additional related facets of relevance.*

CHAPTER 12

AI & LAW: AI IN THE LAW PROJECTS AWRY

Key briefing points about this essay:

- AI in the law continues to grow and mature
- There is AI being used for e-Discovery, for legal contracts analysis, etc.
- Despite the magical semblance, AI consists of software and hardware
- Law practices need to treat AI adoption as a systems implementation project
- Cutting corners or treating the AI project without proper diligence is bad news

Introduction

AI in the law is gaining increasing traction, which also means that there are increased chances of AI projects going awry among law firms pursuing the latest in high-tech systems packed with AI features and functionality.

Let's mindfully explore that assertion.

First, as you assuredly know, there has been a great deal of attention regarding recent and ongoing advances made in AI in the law. Initial steps consist for example of using AI-based Natural Language Processing (NLP) to parse legal text and attempt to interpret the legal meaning and legal nuances in everyday legal contracts. AI advanced search techniques and technologies are being utilized during e-Discovery to analyze large datasets and narrow down the key portions that human attorneys ought to be closely scrutinizing.

And so on.

The hope of someday achieving so-called robo-lawyers is not yet in the cards. In any case, the general aspiration of those developing AI systems is to gradually and inexorably be able to craft machines that can exhibit the equivalent of human intelligence. That being said, please realize that we are a long way away from attaining such a lofty goal. There isn't any kind of AI today that approaches anything even close to sentience and nor is there any clearcut indication we are on the path toward this.

How Law Firm Attempts At AI Go Amiss

When discussing the topic of AI, it is important to keep in mind that we are referring to nothing more than software that runs on some semblance of computer hardware. I say this because the AI moniker oftentimes invokes wild notions of an otherworldly contrivance. The reality is that AI of today is merely an advanced formulation of software that either runs on conventional computer hardware or might utilize specialized hardware devised specifically for AI-based algorithms.

You must dispense entirely from your mind that the aura of AI somehow miraculously also suggests that the AI system is something mystical or magical (a summarily and categorically false impression).

This brings us to the doorstep of wanting to put in place an AI-based legal-oriented system within a law firm. A common catchphrase is to refer to so-called LegalTech as everyday conventional tech used for running a law office and then infuse AI to come up with leading-edge AI-augmented LegalTech.

There is conventional LegalTech that lacks any notable AI augmentation, while there is AI-infused LegalTech that has been amplified by the use of AI functionality (we'll get more into this in a moment). Conventional LegalTech has its pitfalls when being adopted, though enough such squirrely projects have taken place that by and large the gotchas and project dooming traps are relatively well-known. AI projects inherit those potential downfalls and present some added new perils as well.

You might be wondering why some law offices are eager to get into the AI gambit and seek to use the latest in such capabilities.

This spirit of adventure is perhaps laudable and showcases a broader vision of where the law field is heading. Might as well get on board in the early days and not get caught behind the eight ball once AI is pervasive throughout all contemporary law practices.

These early birds are desirous of trying out AI to see whether it does make a difference in their lawyering endeavors. It is the classic aim of boosting the legal team to be more productive, be more efficient, potentially lowering costs, and divining greater billable hours of the legal beagle talent. There is also the notion of attracting new highly sought legal talent to the law practice by proffering that they will be able to leverage the hottest trending capabilities in AI LegalTech.

In terms of informing clients about the fact that AI is being used at a law practice, there is a mixed bag on that score. It could backfire by alarming some clients, such as "what, I don't want some robot doing my legal work" or "I guess my billings should drop to pennies on the dollar since you don't need to use that expensive human labor anymore" (and so on).

Depending upon the types of clients you normally attract, the AI could bolster your image as a state-of-the-art law firm and ergo embellish the image of your practice, or as mentioned it might be confusing or off-putting.

In any case, the question arises about how a law practice can best adopt an AI-based legal-oriented application if they wanted to do so (i.e., best practices for law practices adopting AI).

The odds are that deploying such an app is going to require a hefty amount of upfront preparation, including at times a significant amount of customization or tailoring. Very rarely would you simply do a proverbial plug-and-play into your law practice endeavors (one supposes that if the AI is relatively simplistic, this is somewhat possible, though the AI is not probably going to be especially earthshattering all told).

Okay, let's assume that your own in-house tech team is not going to develop the AI capabilities and that instead, you'll be relying on an outside vendor. Please note that your in-house tech crew will ultimately be asked to aid in supporting the application, which also brings up the importance of integrally including the tech team throughout the entire system adoption process (please don't fall into the throw-it-over-the-wall mentality of surprising the tech crew after the fact, it's a bad approach with equally bad outcomes).

When using an outside vendor for either developing or implementing an AI-based LegalTech application for your practice, make sure to follow all of the advisable precautions that go with any contracted systems effort.

You might find of relevant interest that a project entailing a multi-million dollar customized Contract Lifecycle Management (CLM) system went off the rails and the contracting law firm has filed a lawsuit to cope with the claimed aftermath of an alleged failed implementation (some irony that the particular project entailed automation regarding contract writing, storing, and retrieval).

Law firms have enough legal matters to deal with that accrue billable hours and do not ostensibly want to also tackle their own legal headaches.

According to the filed complaint, the law firm asserts that the project went awry in a myriad of exasperating and costly ways, including claimed failings from A to Z such as inadequate staffing by the software vendor, insufficient initial discovery of the law firm needs, poor design, lack of proper data mapping, lack of proper data conversion, flawed and incomplete documentation, unsatisfactory and incomplete training provided, etc. You can bet that the vendor sees the world differently and a lengthy and distracting legal battle is going to ensue.

The overarching point herein is that an AI-infused legal-oriented app will likely require all of those same elements and more so, thus you need to nail down what the AI capability is going to consist of, along with how it will be established, tested, fielded, and inevitably maintained and updated. If that all seems somewhat obvious, please realize that the allure of AI and the wistfulness of getting a highly sought-after AI-infused LegalTech app seems to make some law partners and their law practice skip blindly past the meat-and-potatoes aspects.

Any software systems vendor worth their salt should be able to layout their AI development or AI implementation methodology (and walk the talk too). This all looks quite similar to conventional systems development or implementation methodologies, albeit tailored to encompass the AI additions. If you don't get that kind of reassuring indication from the vendor, you might want to reconsider them as a viable option.

Just because a particular vendor might not be up to snuff doesn't necessarily mean that the AI aspects are unworkable or otherwise not useful for your law practice. It might just mean that the particular vendor you are wooing or being wooed by is perhaps not sufficiently capable of successfully undertaking the AI infusion.

Conclusion

Some final tips for now.

Do not allow the perceived glamour or innate excitement about being one of the first in your legal niche to add AI into your law office systems to get you into a dreamy state of mind. Remain down to earth, do the due diligence, and treat the system adoption with the attention and care it requires.

Keep your feet firmly planted on the ground when it comes to grabbing the golden ring of AI-infused legal-oriented tech.

.

Note: *For supplemental materials depicting the aspects discussed in this chapter, refer to Appendix B, which contains various augmented diagrams, charts, and additional related facets of relevance.*

CHAPTER 13
AI & LAW:
DOGFOODING FOR AI IN THE LAW

Key briefing points about this article:

- AI in the law continues to grow and mature
- There is AI being used for e-Discovery, for legal contracts analysis, etc.
- Startups are pushing forward on these AI-based LegalTech systems
- They often seek alpha and beta users by cutting deals with outside law firms
- In addition, dogfooding is a handy approach, if suitably arrangeable

Section 1: Introduction

The wheels of progress are turning rapidly in the field of law (perhaps surprisingly so, though mainly in isolated pockets).

AI is increasingly being infused into the law and the practice of law. As you likely know, there has been a great deal of attention regarding recent and ongoing advances made in the adoption of AI into the law.

Initial steps consist for example of using AI-based Natural Language Processing (NLP) to parse legal text and attempt to interpret the legal meaning and legal nuances in everyday legal contracts. AI advanced search techniques and technologies are being utilized during e-Discovery to analyze large datasets and narrow down the key portions that human attorneys ought to be closely scrutinizing. Etc.

There are numerous startups seeking to devise the latest and greatest in marrying AI into carrying out legal tasks via the use of high-tech capabilities. Law firms of all sizes are trying out these AI-infused LegalTech applications.

A typical scenario involves a startup approaching one or more law firms to explore whether they might be willing to serve as an alpha or beta user of the being crafted LegalTech wares. This allows the startup to have a kind of testbed to figure out whether the LegalTech is hitting on all cylinders, and particularly so when incorporating AI capabilities.

The AI part of the system can be the most confounding to get right.

Law firms that open their door to such startup initial forays get an opportunity to first-hand see how the AI-powered LegalTech works. In addition, they potentially have some say in what direction the budding product goes. Of course, there are at times polite (argumentative) debates between what the startup believes the AI ought to do versus what a specific law firm asserts the AI should be doing. Presumably, the startup has to be considering a broader viewpoint of the marketplace all told, rather than any idiosyncrasies of their chosen alpha or beta tryouts.

It turns out there are other paths toward getting early feedback about an in-development AI-based LegalTech system. These additional avenues are somewhat less prevalent and ostensibly rarely considered. Nonetheless, they are worthwhile giving due attention toward. In fact, oftentimes those creating the AI LegalTech app are not aware of these added opportunities to jumpstart their newly devised apps and miss the boat entirely on useful gains.

First, before we venture into the other options, keep in mind that startups are not the only entities seeking to create AI-based LegalTech apps. Law firms themselves are at times launching their own internal efforts to develop such systems. This is usually done in somewhat larger law firms whereby the law practice fortuitously has substantial resources to utilize for considered sideline projects.

For example, a BigLaw firm could readily have an internal R&D group that is asked or proposes to build an AI LegalTech app. The intention typically is to turn the AI app into a product that could be sold to other law firms or licensed to companies containing substantive internal legal departments. You see, the partners of major law firms are often wistfully envisioning a means to more fully balance their portfolio of income-generating sources, going beyond the classic billable hour's mantra alone.

Section 2: Opening New Doors For Testing Purposes

This sets the stage for the added possibilities of getting some of that sorely needed alpha or beta usage during the AI LegalTech development process.

Consider then these added possibilities:

1) A startup opts to use its emerging AI-based LegalTech app as part of their legal efforts
2) A law firm devising an AI LegalTech app opts to try it amid their already proffered legal services

If you have a discerning eye, you might have noticed that those two additional options are both exemplars of *dogfooding*. The notion underlying dogfooding is that a company tries out its internally being devised products by doing so within the firm (which might be the sole path or can be used in concert with outsider testers too).

This is reminiscent of the famous line about being willing to eat your own dog food.

In short, an advantage to testing a budding product within your confines is that doing so will presumably allow for closer tabs on the feedback and keep any adverse responses wholly contained in your own four walls. When using an outsider for such testing efforts, you run the risk of loose lips sinking ships, even when a presumed ironclad non-disclosure agreement is put in place.

Furthermore, the odds are that any evolving AI capability could drive outsiders batty as that portion of the LegalTech system undergoes rapid changes and showcases bugginess. An alpha or beta-using entity is likely to only have so much patience and endurance, reaching a potential boiling point of wanting to drop the effort and leave the AI elements half-done.

As an aside, the origins of the dogfooding catchphrase are somewhat murky, though the customary claimed origin consists of those popular Alpo dog food commercials in the 1970s that featured actor and spokesperson Lorne Greene. The tag line was that not only was the dog food seemingly good for any dogs, but he also fed the dog food to his beloved dogs too.

No better of a testimonial can there be for a product than self-use, one so assumes.

Indeed, anyone developing an AI-based LegalTech app is bound to get asked the direct and unabashed question of whether they are using it themselves. If not, you'd better have a darned good reason why else the assumption is that you aren't willing to eat your own dog food and ergo it must be foul or somehow tainted.

That all being said, the dogfooding approach is not necessarily a bed of roses either.

Internal efforts might only pay lip service to the testing and otherwise eschew getting involved. There is also the chance that internal politics ends up suppressing candid feedback. Some of the testers might figure it is safest to sing high praise, rather than raise alarm bells.

Make sure to weigh the tradeoffs when considering the dogfooding approach.

A startup can mull over whether to use the AI-infused LegalTech for their own internal legal needs, doing so as a dogfooding tactic.

Admittedly, this is a bit of a stretch since the chances of having any substantial in-house legal resources are relatively slim for most startups. The more typical case entails tapping into an external law firm for the bulk of any needed legal services while subsisting as a startup. Using such an already engaged law firm is somewhat a half-in and half-out circumstance, whereby the law firm is obviously an "outsider" while at the same time could be partially construed as a semblance of an insider (kind of).

Either way, it is clear that startups do need to be ready to respond intelligently when asked if they have used the budding product for their legal needs (empty stares are not a good look).

Shifting gears, the more robust case entails a law firm that is crafting an AI-based LegalTech app.

The fairly obvious expectation would be that this ought to be tried out within the entity. If the law firm is not taking that route, there had better be one heck of an explanation and justification. Without something substantive to say about why the product is not being internally tested, many potential buyers or users of the product are apt to be worried that the dog food is unsuitable for everyday consumption.

Section 3: Conclusion

In the computer field, there have been numerous well-known instances of dogfooding avoidance or partial aversion, such as Apple not sufficiently using Apple computers internally and using other choices instead, and likewise, Microsoft not using its wares internally throughout the firm at some stages of their rapid growth.

Bottom-line: Make sure to put dogfooding on your list of considerations and do not get caught doggedly being flatfooted.

Note: *For supplemental materials depicting the aspects discussed in this chapter, refer to Appendix B, which contains various augmented diagrams, charts, and additional related facets of relevance.*

CHAPTER 14
AI & LAW: PRODUCTIZING LEGAL SERVICES VIA AI

Key briefing points about this essay:

- Productization of legal services is a hot trend (aka productization of legal work)
- You take the labor of performing a legal service and shift this into a product
- Most often cited examples include TurboTax and LegalZoom
- Trying to productize is not something you ought to blindly leap into
- Handy tips and insights are provided herein, including leveraging AI aspects

Section 1: Introduction

One of the hottest trends in the legal field entails the energetic rush toward productizing legal services.

Some handily refer to this via the convenient abbreviation of PLS, while others prefer to refer to productizing legal work (PLW). There is nary a notable difference between considering PLS versus PLW, so let's go ahead and treat them as one and the same.

The basic notion underlying this productizing trend is rather straightforward. Rather than seemingly relying solely on proffering legal services, the hope by many is to transform those services into a product reincarnation. In that manner, you can focus on selling a product, doing so in lieu of the daily grind of selling services and dealing with the never-ending slog of garnering labor-oriented billable hours.

Being in a services sector is oftentimes a tough gambit.

You need to find and nurture the expert labor that provides the service. The labor might or might not perform the service in a consistent and reliable manner. Clients of the service might or might not be satisfied with the service. The labor tends to inevitably turnover, and you need to endure the costly effort to bring in new labor and get the labor up-to-speed. And so on.

All of the preceding applies to attorneys and the practice of law. A law practice needs to find and nurture the lawyers brought into the fold. The myriad of attorneys might contain some that do a good job and others that do a poorer job. Clients might or might not be satisfied with the lawyering work done by the attorneys in the practice. Etc.

You get the picture, I'm sure.

Okay, so one alluring means to escape the legal services treadmill would be to convert over to a legal-oriented product. The idea is that a product is something you simply churn out and keep selling. Any labor expended is predominantly toward producing the product and selling the product. The client or customer is usually focused on the product, rather than how the product came to be.

In the legal field, the most commonly cited examples of a successful transformation into a product are the now-famous TurboTax and the equally famed LegalZoom. TurboTax encapsulates the otherwise needed labor of tax experts, while LegalZoom encapsulates the otherwise needed labor of attorneys versed in paperwork matters underlying a plethora of legal forms and contracts.

Those examples illustrate that productization involves taking something that was consuming labor to produce and instead of switching over into promulgating a product that can do the likewise service. I dare say you could assert that a machine is replacing human labor in the circumstances of using a computer system to embody the services knowledge and impart that to customers or clients.

The especially tough part about producing this kind of productization is that you are trying to squeeze out the expertise or knowledge of presumed human experts into becoming a semblance of automation. This can be tricky and not necessarily a slam dunk.

Turns out that the advent of AI capabilities provides keen insights into how to try and take human knowledge and jam it into some form of a computer system. In that sense of things, the emergence of AI in the law is gradually and inexorably taking us down the legal productization path.

For those of you struggling to find ways to shift your legal services into legal products, a smart way to do so includes leveraging the techniques and technologies within the AI in the law rubric.

Section 2: Be Mindful About Productization Of Legal Services

One key aspect of notable clarification, you shouldn't drop everything and leap directly into using AI approaches (or, for that matter, any approaches at all) in order to wantonly pursue productizing legal services or legal work.

Make sure to start at the proper beginning. The best place to start is by considering what legal services or legal work might be the right avenue for you to pursue as a productization candidate. There is a proverbial slogan about this, namely to first identify the problem that needs to be solved, doing so before you launch into an all-consuming effort to do the productization.

If you select the wrong problem to solve, the odds are that anything subsequent that follows, either consciously or via default choice, will be akin to banging your head against a very hard wall. Just because you favor a particular realm of the law or just because you gravitate toward a specific legal practice functional niche does not mean that this is a suitable choice for productizing.

Some of today's legal services are not particularly amendable to productizing. You can get caught trying to push an intractable legal service-oriented boulder up a steep hill and expend a tremendous price in never reaching the desired product pinnacle.

To aid in pinpointing a productization candidate, consider whether the legal services fit into any of these typical process-oriented categories:

- Case Management
- Contracts
- Courts/Trials
- Discovery
- Documents/Records
- Intellectual Property (IP)
- Law Office Activities
- Lawyer/Client Interaction
- Legal Assistants
- Legal Research
- Legal Workflow
- Legal Writing
- Other

Next, consider what area or specialty of the law might be of particular interest, such as:

- Admiralty and Maritime Law
- Appellate Law
- Bankruptcy Law
- Criminal Law
- Estate Planning, Trust and Probate Law
- Family Law
- Franchise and Distribution Law
- Immigration and Nationality Law
- Legal Malpractice Law
- Taxation Law
- Workers' Compensation Law
- Other

You can't boil the entire ocean at once, thus you'll need to select a sufficiently narrow legal focus for your productization endeavors.

Upon exploring a specific and focused arena of legal services, you are ready to gauge whether there are productizing opportunities worth pursuing. This is where the judicious use of AI techniques and technologies can decidedly provide an added edge.

You are looking to uncover what kind of cognition is required when performing the said services. The odds are that some of the services require deep thinking that is going to be a hurdle to replicate in a product format, while other facets are thinkingly routine and lend themselves to being undertaken in AI-based software.

Make sure to differentiate the type of knowledge required when performing the said services. If the knowledge leans toward book learning or similar rendered knowledge, you have an enhanced chance. On the other hand, if the knowledge is seemingly unable to be explicitly articulated, or maybe considered as simply everyday common-sense, these are signs that the productization might be slimly possible.

Of course, you also need to look around and see what competition exists in both the services and the productization of your being considered focus. Will your legal product draw away from the existing services or will those existing services be a greater draw than would your product? Are there legal products already in the market that have shown this to be a viable realm or is it untouched? If untouched, is that because the productization has not yet caught the eyes of others, or is it due to being a considered impossibility?

The usual series of steps can be taken when undertaking a product-producing path. You'll likely need to formulate an entity or business that is driving the productization, which often gives rise to a startup.

What is the business model for this entity?

How will it be funded?

Can you put together a Minimum Viable Product (MVP) to showcase what the product is going to be?

And so on.

Section 3: Conclusion

A notable word of caution about turning legal services into legal products. Looming mighty over these dreamy pursuits is the perilously dangling Damocles sword of the Unauthorized Practice of Law (UPL).

Unlike many other realms of services, the legal field has an atomic bomb, as it were, restricting severely the productization allure. Though some vehemently argue that the unauthorized practice of law is unfairly or unreasonably used at a time, nonetheless it can put the kibosh on the productization you might have in mind.

All told, in the enthusiast and hopeful aims of productizing legal services, keep your feet on the ground and be realistic about what will work and what won't work, for which a smidgeon of knowing about how AI techniques and technologies can be instrumental in turning human knowledge into an automatable form can be a crucial ally on the services-to-product journey.

Note: *For supplemental materials depicting the aspects discussed in this chapter, refer to Appendix B, which contains various augmented diagrams, charts, and additional related facets of relevance.*

CHAPTER 15

AI & LAW: ABA ON LAWYERS KNOWING AI

Key briefing points about this essay:

- AI has become an everyday topic of discussion and is pervasive in our daily lives
- The field of law and the practice of law is increasingly having AI-infused too
- It would seem that not many lawyers are yet up-to-speed about AI in the law
- Few realize too that the ABA proclaimed (kind of) a duty of competence related to AI
- Here is a look at what the ABA says about AI and what lawyers ought to be doing

Section 1: Introduction

What comes to your mind when I mention AI?

It seems that you would ostensibly have to be living in a cave to not be aware that AI is a hot topic these days and that our everyday access to and dependence upon high-tech is becoming increasingly infused with AI.

In some instances, this AI augmentation is welcomed, while in other cases the AI has opened Pandora's box of concerns over computer-based laden biases and inequities.

I would dare assert that most lawyers have heard about AI, along with potentially being subjected to AI-running programs that have impacted their personal lives. For example, perhaps a lawyer seeking a home loan perchance ran afoul of an AI-based mortgage lending app that opted to turn them down for their desired loan. Or maybe a lawyer has used an AI-powered app to help do their annual taxes and tax filings.

That being said, the realistic odds are though that relatively few lawyers are aware of how AI intertwines with the law and the practice of law.

Yes, sadly, lawyers are often so focused on the daily treadmill of generating billable hours that they have little time or energy to be thinking about AI in the law.

You might be therefore interested in knowing what the ABA has to say about lawyers needing to know about AI in the practice of law. In short, lawyers are supposed to know about the present and future of AI in the law. Ironically, of a sort, not only don't lawyers generally know about AI In the law, but they are also unaware that they are supposed to diligently know about the topic, as so proclaimed for their complying with the official lawyering standards and practices promulgated by the ABA.

That's a double whammy, namely not knowing about AI in the law and additionally not knowing that they are supposed to know about the very thing they don't know about (a tongue twister and conundrum, for sure).

Let's start by briefly identifying how AI comes to play in the practice of law. After doing so, we will take a close look at the ABA stated indications on this lawyering ought-to-know topic.

AI in the law is still in its infancy. Initial steps consist for example of using AI-based Natural Language Processing (NLP) to parse legal text and attempt to interpret the legal meaning and legal nuances in everyday legal contracts. AI advanced search techniques and technologies are being utilized during e-Discovery to analyze large datasets and narrow down the key portions that human attorneys ought to be closely scrutinizing.

And so on.

You can bet your bottom dollar that AI is already starting to be found in and will largely eventually overtake the high-tech used to do case management, contracts development and upkeep, discovery, client interaction and communique, court prep and trial assistance, legal research and analyses, etc. Inch by inch, those applications and so-called LegalTech will embody AI capabilities that make the software easier to use and take on some portions of the lawyering task at hand.

All of those aspects are dealing with the application of AI to the practice of law.

There is yet another side to the AI-in-the-law coin.

You see, there are two major ways to mix together AI and the law: (1) AI as applied to the law and the practice of law, (2) Law as applied to the advent of AI. Thus, lawyers need to be ready and competently able to use AI within their law firms and throughout the adjudication process. Plus, lawyers need to become knowledgeable about the laws and governance related to AI systems and be able to proffer sound legal advice accordingly to their clients that are using or impacted by AI systems.

Okay, that sets the stage for the overarching indication by the ABA pertaining to this matter.

Here's what the ABA has summarily stated: "RESOLVED, That the American Bar Association urges courts and lawyers to address the emerging ethical and legal issues related to the usage of artificial intelligence ("AI") in the practice of law including: (1) bias, explainability, and transparency of automated decisions made by AI; (2) ethical and beneficial usage of AI; and (3) controls and oversight of AI and the vendors that provide AI" (per American Bar Association, House of Delegates, Resolution adopted on August 12-13, 2019).

Some attorneys, upon reading this ABA pronouncement, will merely shrug their shoulders and contend that since the resolution merely "urges" lawyers (an interpretatively soft phrasing) this allows for more than enough leeway to stridently argue that it is altogether a vague and weakly worded declaration, meaning that no sane lawyer has to worry about the proclamation.

Case closed.

One supposes that you could choose to ignore the ABA statement if you desired to do so. Furthermore, you could likely also use as an escape hatch the claim that you didn't even know that the resolution existed (it is admittedly rather obscure, somewhat hidden from conventional view). In that sense, you can use the infamous variant of the Chewbacca defense that ignorance is bliss.

A contrary view is that taking such a stance could be construed as a wink-wink momentary avoidance tactic, such that eventually you'll need to get familiar with AI in the law, and meanwhile will blindly tread along realizing that it is just a someday (maybe) item on your pending To-Do list.

Section 2: More To Say And More To Know

As further meat to the bones, as it were, the ABA also published an article entitled "Artificial Intelligence And The Law: The ABA's Important And Timely Contribution" which came out around the same timeframe as the posted resolution (the article was published on August 26, 2019).

On a related tangent, a quick question that might come to your mind is whether the ABA statement and the corresponding ABA article are still worth their salt, given that they were posted in 2019. The answer is absolutely and abundantly yes. The same foundational points made in 2019 are equally of importance today.

As a small caveat, I would politely suggest that there are even more topics to be encompassed, due to the further advances made in AI and the practice of law, but the earlier narrative is still viable and fully apt.

The ABA article provides a slew of questions that AI-astute lawyers ought to know how to respond. Here are some of those meaty questions for you to consider: "Questions abound: to what extent may my clients use impenetrable, potentially biased algorithms to make determinations that assess or affect customers or unsuspecting citizens? What should they disclose? What representations can my clients fairly make about the AI solutions they market? Should my firm use AI in recruiting? Is AI more accurate than conventional approaches in complying with data subject access requests under GDRP and CCPA? Can I sufficiently trust AI in e-discovery to make representations to the court – or to determine case strategy?"

Speaking of lawyer competencies, the ABA article notes this: "The resolution correctly recognizes, referencing Rule 1.1 of the ABA Model Rules (Duty of Competence), that attorneys must 'be informed, and up to date, on current technology.' It also underscores that attorneys 'cannot be expected to know all the technical intricacies of AI systems." (per the ABA article).

Ponder for a moment the latter part of that quotation.

One of the easiest excuses used by lawyers that are aiming to look the other way when it comes to learning about AI In the law consists of exhorting that they don't have the time and nor inclination to learn the *technical intricacies* of AI. That seems like a bona fide excuse. But, either that excuse is based on a false understanding of what they need to actually know, or it is a cleverly devised sidelining argument to distract from the crux of the matter.

The point is that lawyers do not need to know about the technical intricacies of AI and ergo it is a false pretext to bandy around.

Knowing the technical intricacies is decidedly not what the intention is and nor is it a necessity either. Instead, the notion is to ensure familiarity with what AI consists of, what its limits are, how it is used, how it is improperly used, all within a legal context.

No need to delve into bits and bytes, and no need to carry around a screwdriver or high-tech-related accouterments.

Of course, to further clarify, lawyers are welcomed to dig more deeply into AI and discover the technical intricacies, if of interest and relevance to their personal and professional interests (this is not a requirement and should not be alleged as such).

One final point for now.

The ABA article rightfully posits a serious criticism of a kind about the ABA pronouncement.

Recall that the resolution is notably succinct, and as such has a severely lacking element: "But it falls short of asking a crucial question: What constitutes evidence of competence for use of AI in the legal system?" (per the ABA article).

Section 3: Conclusion

Sometimes, something that is short and sweet is not enough. To add teeth to the matter, the hope is that the ABA will ultimately stipulate particulars concerning AI-related lawyering competencies. Until then, lawyers are on the honor system.

You can choose whether to abide by a classic wait-and-see attitude, only being dragged into AI in the law when the dangling sword of compliance becomes clearer, or perhaps you'll be forced anyway into the AI-in-the-law tsunami as you are swept along by your peers and the courts and society all told.

At this juncture, the choice is yours as you see fit.

Note: *For supplemental materials depicting the aspects discussed in this chapter, refer to Appendix B, which contains various augmented diagrams, charts, and additional related facets of relevance.*

CHAPTER 16
AI & LAW:
LAW SCHOOLS AI COURSES

Key briefing points about this essay:

- AI in the law is gaining speed throughout the legal profession
- One focus consists of using AI-based tools for undertaking lawyering tasks
- Another focus involves helping clients that are dealing with AI system legal issues
- Some assert that law schools need to do more toward AI in the law for their students
- A recent study of U.S. law schools examined their AI-in-the-law course offerings

Section 1: Introduction

A recent study has helpfully identified the extent to which there are various courses on Law and Artificial Intelligence that are being offered at law schools throughout the United States.

As a side note, it is considered herein equivalent to construe that this overall realm is equally expressed as "Law and Artificial Intelligence" or as "Artificial Intelligence and Law" and no distinction is made here between the sequencing of those wordings. I mention this because some do consider those two phrasings as having a different meaning (the study that I am referring to does not, thankfully so).

Allow me a momentary tangent to explain the wording confusion that sometimes arises, which is also beneficial to the gist of this discussion in any case.

You see, there are two major ways to intertwine AI and the law: (1) AI as applied to the law and the practice of law, (2) Law as applied to the advent of AI.

In the first case, lawyers need to be ready and competently able to use AI within their law firms and throughout the adjudication process. Think of LegalTech that is infused with AI capabilities, such as AI aiding e-Discovery or AI that analyzes legal contracts. In the second case, lawyers need to become knowledgeable about the laws and governance related to AI systems and be able to proffer sound legal advice accordingly to their clients that are using or impacted by AI systems. Think of regulatory actions and newly passed laws dealing with AI systems that contain laden and untoward biases and inequities.

Unfortunately, some try to muddle things by contending that "Artificial Intelligence and Law" refers to the first case, while "Law and Artificial Intelligence" refers to the second case. I find this to be onerous and unneeded, plus it is just plain confusing to most everyday readers. In my view, any mention of AI and law, or the phrasing of law and AI, refer to the totality of intermixing the two domains and ergo encompasses both ways of mixing them together.

Now, back to the main event.

For anyone tracking the advent of AI in the law, this recent and notably handy study undertook a quite extensive look at how widespread the teaching about legal-oriented aspects of AI is now becoming in law schools.

You might have assumed that such courses have been taking place extensively already, given that AI has become a big-time headline-grabbing topic in today's society, but you would be wrong.

Generally, offering a course specifically dealing with AI in the law has been a rarity in law schools. If it has been offered, it is usually erratically offered and only takes place from time to time. When a faculty member perchance has a particular interest in the AI and law topic, they often take up the mantle and offer such a class. This interest can though eventually wear out and end up being a hit-or-miss proposition underlying the offering of the course.

On top of this, law school students are often unsure of whether to take a course on AI in the law, even if it is offered. One common assumption is that the course must be only for techie-oriented law school students, thus this presumption immediately reduces the pool of students seeking such a class (this techie notion is usually not the case). In addition, law school students tend to weigh the value of any optional courses against the expected impact on their budding legal-oriented careers. As such, it is sadly unlikely at this time that many law firms give bonus points or special attention to law students that have taken an AI in the law class (this is gradually changing, inexorably and inevitably).

Section 2: The Study Tells All

Let's dig into the study and see what it found.

The results indicated that about one-quarter of law schools surveyed appear to have a class relatively devoted to the AI in the law topic. I say "devoted" as distinguishing between law school classes that perchance have a minor mention of AI and those classes that principally seem to encompass AI legal-oriented facets.

Here's how the researchers described their study findings: "Based on this review of all published Law & AI course offerings in ABA approved law schools in the United States, we find that, through the 2019–20 academic year, 26% of the approximately top 200 ranked U.S. law schools offer (or recently offered) a Law & AI course. But only 13% of schools appear to offer more than one Law & AI course" (as per authors Brendan Johnson and Francis Shen, "Teaching Law and Artificial Intelligence" in the Minnesota Journal of Law, Science & Technology, Volume 22, Issue 2, 2021).

The method used to count the courses consisted of this indicated approach: "To identify current and recent law school courses focused on Law & AI, we operationalized 'recent' to include any courses offered in the past five years, i.e., since the Spring 2016 Semester. We defined a course as 'focused on Law & AI' as any course in which at least one-third of the course was devoted to issues at the intersection of law & AI." Furthermore, their research was primarily based on website info: "With these search criteria, we examined the web sites for each of 197 law schools listed in the U.S. News and World Report rankings list with publicly available course catalogs" (they then did additional follow-up with the law schools offering AI in the law classes).

To some modest degree, this approach might undercount the actual number of such courses, which is an inherent study limitation as noted by the researchers. Also, the study focuses exclusively on U.S. law schools and does not, therefore, include other the law schools of other countries.

In any case, some illuminating facets of this very worthwhile study are:

- There seemed to be a pattern of higher-ranked law schools tending to be more likely to offer AI in the law courses than lower-ranked law schools.

- Law schools that are offering AI in the law courses tended to also be more consistently known for their scholarly efforts in the AI in the legal realm.

- Overview-oriented courses on AI in the law tended to be predominant, rather than specially focused classes such as within a niche of the law (e.g., IP and AI) or a niche in AI (e.g., cybersecurity and law).

- Relatively few of the classes used an assigned textbook, apparently resorting to using articles or other materials as sources for the law students to study.

- Most of the classes were offered for two credits, though there were one credit and three credit varieties also frequently occurring.

Finally, the researchers provided four key recommendations, all of which I abundantly agree with and that I have somewhat rephrased in my own words here:

- Every law school should have at least one course in AI and the law (and, for which it should preferably be a survey or overview-oriented class, plus the course should be regularly and consistently offered).

- Law schools should also offer topic-specific courses that cover a niche of AI in the law, providing an opportunity to more deeply dive into the said topic, which an overview course would normally not entail.

- Increased attention to the interdisciplinary collaboration between law schools and their collegially aligned departments such as computer science, engineering, and the like should be pursued to strengthen the AI in the law courses and bolster research and scholarship in this realm.

- Rankings of law schools should include or even be focused entirely on whether AI in the law courses is being offered at the law school. In particular, the authors advocate a U.S. News and World Report new ranking category of Best Law & AI Programs be instituted.

That fourth point about rankings being reworked to include whether AI in the law is being taught is the likeliest way to prod law schools into taking action on this topic. Without some skin in the game, which is what rankings can garner, the odds are that many law schools will not get off the dime and try to incorporate AI in the law into their curriculums.

Of course, you cannot necessarily blame law schools for perhaps lagging on the AI in the law course offerings gambit. Until the legal marketplace clamors for law graduates having AI in the law under their belt, there is little incentive for law schools to provide such classes. Keep in mind too that there are lots of other competing forces trying to get law schools to offer courses on all kinds of topics. There is a continual push and pull that makes life particularly difficult for law schools when it comes to deciding on the courses to be offered.

Another key factor is finding faculty suitable to teach an AI in the law class. Few of the faculty at a law school is bound to be versed in AI. They then either have to expend energy and precious attention to come up-to-speed or try to offer a class that they feel uneasy teaching. You can anticipate that the personal cost to prepare for and undertake such a new class is probably not going to glean any special compensation or meritorious value for the faculty member.

It is a bit of a conundrum.

One means of expediting the AI in the law as a course offering is by leveraging one of the other recommendations that were made, namely by doing so collaboratively with a colleague that is versed in AI such as from the computer science or engineering programs. This helps, though it also means having to get approvals from two separate bureaucracies and deal with other potential difficulties.

Section 3: Conclusion

Let's end with an upbeat message.

With just a quarter or so of law schools in the U.S. currently offering an AI in the law class, the sky is the limit. Keep your eye on the numbers since the chances are that AI in the law will become an increasingly hot trend and we might very well see growth to half of the law schools and someday nearly all law schools offering such a class.

Admittedly, that might be a glass is half full perspective.

.

Note: *For supplemental materials depicting the aspects discussed in this chapter, refer to Appendix B, which contains various augmented diagrams, charts, and additional related facets of relevance.*

CHAPTER 17

AI & LAW: AI MISTAKES BY LAW AUTHORS

Key briefing points about this essay:

- AI in the law is gaining speed throughout the legal profession
- Articles about AI in the law are increasingly appearing and being sought
- By and large, these are usually written by legal-oriented authors
- This in turn typically reveals that the AI side of the discussions are rather weak
- Here is what to watch out for and hopefully improve in that regard

Section 1: Introduction

There are a rising number of articles getting published and article submissions being submitted that aim to cover the expanding and rapidly innovating field of AI in the law.

That's a good thing.

AI-in-the-law needs to evolve and mature.

Lots of creative and fascinating twists and turns are being explored, gradually establishing AI-in-the-law as a fertile area for both academic and practitioner merits. Think of this as a handy double whammy, namely you can contribute to the field of law and you can contribute to the field of AI, all in one fell swoop.

The bad news is that those with a predominantly legal-only background are oftentimes dropping the ball or at least undermining the presumed law-and-AI duality proposition by doing a notably lousy or altogether disappointing job on the AI part of the AI-in-the-law pairing.

As a frequent reviewer of journal-submitted articles and likewise in my capacity as serving on editorial boards and being an associate editor too, I have come across quite a number of earnest submissions about AI-in-the-law that are regrettably undercut by the lack of AI savviness imbued into the piece by well-meaning but missing-the-mark legal-oriented authors.

You see, oftentimes a legal researcher or even a legal practitioner puts together an interesting and perhaps publishable worthy article that unfortunately falls apart on the AI side of things. By and large, the legal or law field elements of the submission are usually solidly constructed. This makes sense since the primary expertise of the author (or authors) is typically in the legal realm.

Meanwhile, such authors seem to believe that if they perchance toss some semi-random quotes from a seemingly reputable AI-focused journal piece or acclaimed AI scholar as their cited source for discussing how AI and the law intertwine, this is enough to get them a free pass. Indeed, amazingly, the paper might pass with flying colors when reviewed solely by a law journal that employs exclusively law-oriented peer reviewers.

Please know that if that same submission came under the scrutiny of a true AI expert or scholar on Artificial Intelligence, the piece would likely take heavy blows and undergo a dutifully appropriate withering attack. The article would not get approved for an AI journal, until or if the authors took a more strident line on the AI aspects.

It seems that some legal-oriented authors somehow believe (or assume) that they can read a few articles about AI and suddenly become ostensibly bona fide experts about AI. Or that if they cherry-pick an AI article or two from a reputable AI-focused journal, this alone is sufficient to cover themselves when discussing AI topics in the context of AI in the law.

Allow me to put the shoe on the other foot, showcasing how exasperating this can be.

Suppose an author that was imminently well-versed in computer science and AI were to decide to write a journal article about AI and the law. Assume that this person has very little knowledge about the law. Nonetheless, they cherry-pick from one or two bona fide law pub articles, trying to make their submission seem endowed with pristine and robust legal ramifications.

The odds are that a legal-oriented reviewer that knows what they are doing would quickly slice and dice the submission, pointing out the lack of rigorous understanding of the law.

I'll point out in fairness that the article might get approved by an AI journal, albeit doing the same one-sided reviewing as what the law journals tend to do. In essence, if the AI was good enough, and if the reviewers were AI people, they would not give much attention to the law side of the piece and just go with the flow that it must be apt and accurate.

This is precisely the same kind of mistake made by legal-oriented authors that try to sneak under the radar by infusing AI aspects into their submission to legal-oriented journals. Depending upon how careful the law journal is, the lack of AI validity and intelligible intermixing might go completely unscathed, and the article will get approved (based presumably and nearly solely on the legal-oriented portions about the law).

For those legal-oriented authors that are pretty much happy with skating through by being astute on the law but severely weak on the AI side, I suppose you can just keep doing what you are doing already. No need to try and dig more deeply into the AI aspects. I would though personally hope for more fortitude on such matters.

That being said, as the field of AI in the law matures, the odds are that the barrier to entry will heighten, based on more and more reviewers that are seriously ingrained in AI and also in the law. How long you have to continue the strong on the law and weak on the AI as an intertwining might be a shorter runway than you think.

Section 2: Showing What Not To Do And Why

With all of that exhortation about the failings associated with the AI elements in many of the AI in the law articles, you might be keenly interested to know what kinds of pitfalls I'm referring to. I'm glad that you asked.

To keep this discussion somewhat brief, I'll cover four of the most commonly observed weaknesses or undercutting by those that are genuinely pursuing AI-in-the-law and perchance are strong on the law but weak on the AI.

I provide this as a helpful and heartfelt encouragement for uplifting further the gestalt of the AI-in-the-law realm as both a scholarly pursuit and as a budding profession:

1) Not recognizing that AI in the law is a two-sided coin

Let's back up a moment and consider what it means when writing about AI in the law.

You see, there are two major ways to intertwine AI and the law: (1) AI as applied to the law and the practice of law, (2) Law as applied to the advent of AI.

In the first case, lawyers and legal scholars emphasize the use of AI as applied to the law, which I'll signify as the so-called robo-lawyer, robo-judge, robo-juror, and the like. I am not a fan of that verbiage, but it is admittedly a quick way to invoke the imagery of what applied AI is ultimately aiming to perhaps do. At this time, those robo-legal contrivances do not yet exist in any semblance of what they imply. Think instead of LegalTech that is infused with AI capabilities, such as AI aiding e-Discovery or AI that analyzes legal contracts, etc.

In the second case, lawyers and legal scholars emphasize the laws and governance related to AI systems. What should regulators be doing and not be doing about the advent of AI in our society? How should attorneys advise their clients when those clients are crafting, fielding, or utilizing AI-based systems? Think of regulatory actions and newly passed laws dealing with AI systems that contain laden and untoward biases and inequities as the most headline-grabbing AI-governance issues of the moment.

Any genuine article on AI in the law ought to clarify which side of the coin the article is intending to discuss and presumably advance in some manner. If you don't mention this, it leaves any savvy reader waiting on pins and needles to discern what your focus is. Also, if you cover just one side of the coin, it could suggest that you aren't even aware that there are two sides involved (I'm not saying you need to cover both sides, only acknowledge that both sides do in fact exist).

2) Pinning your AI understanding on simplistic views of what AI constitutes

I have seen countless instances of using merely one quoted definition of AI as the proclaimed and seemingly all-knowing heralded definition of AI, as though the quote is irrefutably right. The reality is that there is a great deal of open debate about what AI per se constitutes.

I've written extensively about the difficulties that regulators, lawmakers, and AI scholars are having about defining AI into newly devised laws. Any meaty AI-in-the-law paper that doesn't acknowledge and try to address this morass is skirting around the meat and potatoes by trying to do handwaving about what AI is (usually, this is done as a purposeful, say sneaky, set up to make the article more easily able to cover the legal topic at hand).

Imagine if you were reading a law journal article about an entire subfield of the law and the author opted to delve into an entire body of law by using just a simple one-sentence descriptor. I am sure it would cause you to shake your head and become skeptical about what the author and the paper have to say about that specific subfield of law.

The same can be said about the AI portion of an AI-in-the-law article.

3) Relying on a one-sided singular AI expert or scholar as the basis for what AI is

Lawyers and legal scholars are indubitably clever. I say this in a complimentary way. This also means that to deal with what AI constitutes is, the usual trick involves picking a known AI expert or scholar and quoting them. Voila, problem solved. In theory, nobody can attack your AI infusion since it is taken verbatim from a recognized AI intellectual.

Case closed.

Though this does seem to solve the matter, it really just puts your skates onto thin ice. I assure you that whatever the AI expert has said, there are likely other equally credible AI experts that in some manner disagree or have an alternative viewpoint on whatever the quote indicates.

You have essentially played a trick on the unknowing legal-steeped reviewers and readers. They don't realize that the quoted AI expert is not the end-all-be-all. The assumption is that the quote must be ironclad and rock solid.

I oftentimes need to remind those in the legal field that there is nearly always a counterargument that coincides with any argued point (something otherwise readily known and daily experienced by those immersed in the law). The same is true for AI and the field of AI. Find me one acclaimed AI expert and give me a quote, and I can undoubtedly find a retort or counterargument.

By conveniently leaving out such a counterargument amidst your submission, nobody would seem to be the wiser (other than if it was being scrutinized by someone that really knew the AI field).

4) Getting into the rut of assuming that AI is only what AI is as of today

This final point, for now, is one that really takes the cake and can be considered endemic throughout many AI-in-the-law discussions.

Here's how it goes.

You mention that Machine Learning is a hot topic in today's AI field. You then equate that all of AI is entirely subsumed within the rubric of Machine Learning. Thus, you make the hidden and insidious portrayal that AI is entirely and only consisting of Machine Learning.

Furthermore, adding insult to injury, as it were, the author suggests or silently implies that Machine Learning as we know of it in current times is what Machine Learning will always be.

For those that relish having an easy strawman to then tackle, this is the way to get there. Easy-peasy. You can then just jump into the foray and mention all of the already known limitations and weaknesses of Machine Learning. Meanwhile, the implication is that this is assuredly true for all of AI.

And, the added implication is that this is true for AI as we will know of it tomorrow.

But this flies in the face of ongoing advances and likely breakthroughs that will occur in the AI field. To assume that the AI or today, or the subset of AI known as Machine Learning (of today), will be the same in say five years, ten years, fifty years, seems a rather questionable assumption (plus, it ought to be overtly stated, if that's what you are claiming will happen).

In my work, I've explicitly laid out that there are several distinctive Levels of Autonomy (LoA) for AI capabilities, and we are only in the earlier stages at this time. Assuming that we gradually advance, you are missing the mark by trying to blanket all AI with whatever criticisms or limitations you are divining. It would be better to clearly state that you are focusing on the AI of today and ergo acknowledge there is an AI of tomorrow.

Your criticisms of AI of today might not be applicable or be differently arising in later Levels of Autonomy of AI.

Of course, the trick that some take is to play a dirty game, employing the sometimes trickery of a classic crafty legal argumentation ploy. You make it seem like there is either the AI of today or there is the sci-fi sentient AI of tomorrow. By casting this as a mutually exclusive dichotomy, you can knock down the sci-fi variant as unreasonable and farfetched. This neatly makes your focus on the AI of today seem completely right-headed (versus having to deal with a graduating set of Levels of Autonomy of AI).

The AI strawman gambit is a thing of beauty and pulls the wool over most eyes, woefully so.

Section 3: Conclusion

There is a lot more to be said about many other additional traps, which I'll aim to cover in subsequent discussions. Let's, for now, consider a few concluding remarks.

Some legal-oriented authors are utterly unaware of falling into these kinds of traps. When presented with these faltering ways, they usually sheepishly see the merits of taking a stronger stance toward the AI portions of their AI-in-the-law endeavors. I applaud them.

Other legal-oriented authors that are made aware of these questionable practices are at times upset, defending strenuously whatever they may have done, regardless that these traps do seemingly exist in their work. For them, I wish them continued good luck and regret if any of this might seem disconcerting.

For those legal-oriented authors that have done their work such that it is both strong on the law and strong on the AI side, I appreciate the dutiful approach undertaken. That's what we need to ensure that the AI-in-the-law field gains steam and becomes the enriched arena that it promises to establish.

A solid AI-in-the-law milieu will do well for everyone concerned, hitting high marks for AI and likewise attaining high marks in the law.

Note: *For supplemental materials depicting the aspects discussed in this chapter, refer to Appendix B, which contains various augmented diagrams, charts, and additional related facets of relevance.*

CHAPTER 18

AI & LAW: ARTIFICIAL COMPLEX LITIGATION

Key briefing points about this essay:

- AI in the law is gaining speed and there is little doubt of a rising trajectory
- Usual ways of applying AI include e-Discovery, doing legal contracts analyses, etc.
- Another potential focus would be in aiding litigations, especially complex ones
- Recent research highlights four key roles of AI in litigation matters
- There are both merits to using AI in litigation and caveats to be noted too

Section 1: Introduction

The various ways in which AI is being applied to the law seemingly know no bounds.

There are ongoing and innovative twists and turns that are finding new avenues of applying AI for legally sound and substantive means, presumably doing so to bolster lawyering and more so assist throughout the totality of everyday adjudication and jurisprudence.

You likely already know about especially popular uses of AI in the law such as infusing Natural Language Processing (NLP) capabilities into the arduous chore of doing e-Discovery (i.e., AI-based NLP is especially useful when dealing with large-scale narrative-oriented datasets that require extensive and otherwise laborious by-hand legal discovery efforts). And you are perhaps familiar with the use of AI for aiding in examining and composing legal contracts.

The list of AI applied uses goes on and on.

One quick aside.

Please know that there are two major ways to intertwine AI and the law: (1) AI as applied to the law and the practice of law, (2) Law as applied to the advent of AI. In the first case, lawyers and legal scholars emphasize the use of AI as applied to the law, which I'll signify as the so-called robo-lawyer, robo-judge, robo-juror, and the like kinds of aspirations. Note that I am not a fan of that robo verbiage, but it is admittedly a quick way to invoke the imagery of what applied AI is ultimately aiming to do.

In the second case, lawyers and legal scholars emphasize the laws and governance related to AI systems. This is best illustrated by a few example questions that are being wrestled with these days. For example, what should regulators be doing and not be doing about the advent of AI in our society? How should attorneys advise their clients when those clients are crafting, fielding, or utilizing AI-based systems? Think of regulatory actions and newly passed laws dealing with AI systems that contain laden and untoward biases and inequities as the most headline-grabbing AI-governance issues of the moment.

Section 2: Keeping The List Of Applied AI-In-The-Law Well-Maintained And Updated

A recent article by legal scholar Joshua Davis at the University of San Francisco School of Law provides some fascinating added ways in which we can inevitably expect AI to be applied to the law (the paper is scheduled to appear in the *Hastings Law Journal*).

The focus on the additional roles for AI stems from a close-up look at the complexities of litigation. It is reasonable to anticipate that we will gradually see AI increasingly being used as a vital tool for performing a myriad of legal tasks associated with litigation-related lawyering, particularly when the complexity of the litigation raises to a level that such AI augmentation would be likely worthwhile.

For sake of discussion, this might be referred to by using a handy catchphrase such as Artificial Complex Litigation (ACL) or perhaps known simply overall as AI-augmented litigation. The latter naming removes the wording of being necessarily complex, denoting that we might equally find beneficial the use of AI in a wide range of litigation matters, ranging from the easiest instances to the hardest or most complex cases. The usage depends upon how costly or burdensome the AI capability might be, weighed against the nature of the case and what the AI might constructively glean or produce.

There are four major roles that are specifically delved into via the insightful paper:

"(1) **Strategic Advice**—providing strategic advice to litigants and parties;
(2) **Advocacy**—advocating before a judge or jury;
(3) **Class Action Settlement Assessments**—assisting a judge in deciding whether to approve class action settlements; and
(4) **Proposing or Imposing Compromise**—assessing the average result of legal action, potentially as a benchmark for settlement or as a standard for imposing a result in arbitration."

Let's briefly unpack each of those four roles.

Consider first the role of AI in providing strategic advice during litigation.

Imagine that there are litigants and lawyers battling over a case that might seem otherwise intractable and perhaps is being ardently fueled by raw emotion to some degree between the key parties. The AI could potentially serve as a kind of impartial actor that could reduce the fury of the case and allow for a more even-keeled look at things.

One side might consult an AI system to gauge whether the odds of winning the case are viable. By doing so, perhaps this side of the case opts to settle the matter or at least pursue such a possibility. Of course, both sides might consult with the AI, and there is also the notion that the AI would aid toward finding a reasoned and agreeable way to generally conclude the litigation without further extended legal action.

As mentioned by Davis, the AI could "provide a more reliable empirical basis for strategic decisions" and shift attention to facts and figures, shifting away from the usual heightened passions involved. The idea too is that this form of AI ought to customize rather than be routinized, thus being able to fit the particulars of the litigation. This can be applied in a rather extensive manner. Envision that when a case goes to court, the AI might be advising an attorney as to their strategy in the courtroom, such as aiming to "tailor those recommendations to particular judges and jurors" (showcasing a degree of deepness beyond just generic stock kinds of legal-related guidance).

Moving onward to the second of the four identified roles, we can readily anticipate that AI could serve in a legal-oriented advocacy capacity. Per the paper: "AI may someday synthesize legal sources, evidence, allegations, or the like in a written form that maximizes the chances of a desired outcome. It may do so by appealing not only to a judge's values but also to her biases and confusions. In this regard, too, AI may exploit information about a judge, perhaps from public records, including past judicial proceedings, and perhaps from her online activities, much of which is or may be for sale."

The third mentioned role entails aiding the settlement of class actions. Judges oftentimes have an especially tough time trying to weigh the various merits and positions entangling class litigation. Davis suggests that AI might come to the fore: "A judge could use its analysis of the likely outcomes of litigation and their odds of occurring. That could assist a judge in gauging the relationship between a settlement and what might be expected to happen on average in litigation."

Finally, the fourth role encompasses the challenges in trying to find a compromise that will get litigants to consider a mutually agreeable resolution. The AI itself might act in a type of mediator or arbitrator capacity: "AI could go beyond advising, advocating, and assisting. It could offer an alternative form
of dispute resolution. We might call it expected value (EV) mediation or arbitration."

Section 3: Conclusion

Be aware that none of the preceding uses of AI are without some concomitant reservations and inherent limitations.

The paper rightfully points out that each of the AI roles will have downsides. The AI could inadvertently make matters worse and somehow spark the litigants into greater ferocity. There might be appeals made that would clog our courts, based on having to figure out what did the AI do and whether the AI was biased or rigged in some fashion.

As they say, when using AI, sometimes you live by the sword, but you can also die by the sword. That is the harsh reality associated with any high-tech tool, AI or otherwise. Without seeming to be a doom and gloom purveyor, the ways in which especially AI in the law can go awry is probably as endless as the way in which AI is going to be applied to the law.

One supposes that the good news, of a sort, highlights my earlier point that there are two ways to intertwine AI and the law. Some lawyers will use AI to aid their legal cases. Other lawyers will be called upon to litigate cases involving questions about what the AI did or did not do. Whichever way you get involved, AI is here to stay and will be immersed in the professional lives of lawyers in a quite immersive manner.

.

Note: *For supplemental materials depicting the aspects discussed in this chapter, refer to Appendix B, which contains various augmented diagrams, charts, and additional related facets of relevance.*

CHAPTER 19
AI & LAW:
LEGAL GOALS AND OBJECTIVES

Key briefing points about this essay:

- AI in the law is gaining speed and increasingly being applied to many legal uses
- Usual ways of applying AI include e-Discovery, doing legal contracts analyses, etc.
- Some legal researchers mention that setting legal goals and objective is an issue
- In essence, the claim is that AI cannot set its own legal directives, unlike humans
- This is a useful argument worthy of exploring and noting counterarguments too

Section 1: Introduction

How are you at setting ostensibly proper and robust sets of legal goals and objectives when it comes to legal cases that you undertake?

According to prudent methods of practicing law, you presumably take a contemplative moment or two when first laying out a legal case that has come to your attention and aim to derive a suitable set of legal goals and objects for the case at hand. This provides a kind of North Star, as it were, serving as an overarching form of guidance throughout the likely murkiness and muck of any everyday grinding legal matters of a case. You can keep your head on straight by referring back to the earlier established legal goals and objectives.

Not every lawyer necessarily takes the notion of setting legal goals and objectives to heart.

There are some seasoned lawyers that say it is a waste of time to write out anything of such a nature. They would contend that the odds are a legal case is going to have so many twists and turns that any initial legal goals and objectives will be no longer viable and ergo useless. Another viewpoint by some attorneys is that you simply use your gut instinct about legal goals and objectives. Apparently, in a somewhat smarmy attitude, the implication is that only newbie attorneys take the time to compose case-based legal goals and objectives (doing so because they haven't yet earned their lawyering stripes, seemingly).

My opening question to you was whether you perchance set legal goals and objectives. In addition, I've heightened the question by asking too whether the legal goals and objectives are stridently proper and robust. In that sense, even if you do establish legal goals and objectives, there can be quite a difference between hastily or shoddy ones and a set that is more carefully and mindfully crafted.

I won't belabor the point and instead will shift to a completely different angle that might catch you a bit off-guard.

As we continue to see more and more AI being applied to the law, some are wondering what the basis for establishing suitable legal goals and objectives will be.

I realize that might seem ambiguous or confounding, so let's back up and first clarify the overall aspects of AI being applied to the law. We'll then return to the matter of legal goals and objectives.

You likely already know about especially popular ways of applying AI in the law such as infusing Natural Language Processing (NLP) capabilities into the arduous chore of doing e-Discovery (i.e., AI-based NLP is especially useful when dealing with large-scale narrative-oriented datasets that require extensive and otherwise laborious by-hand legal discovery efforts). And you are perhaps familiar with the use of AI for aiding in examining and composing legal contracts.

The list of such AI-applied uses is continually growing.

Please also know that there are two major ways to intertwine AI and the law: (1) AI as applied to the law and the practice of law, (2) Law as applied to the advent of AI. In the first case, which is the focus of this discussion, lawyers and legal scholars emphasize the use of AI as applied to the law, which I'll signify as the so-called robo-lawyer, robo-judge, robo-juror, and the like kinds of aspirations. Note that I am not a fan of that robo verbiage, but it is admittedly a quick way to invoke the imagery of what applied AI is ultimately aiming to do.

Section 2: Who Or What Will Be Setting Legal Goals And Objectives

Now that we've set the stage for our discussion, let's jump into the legal goals and objectives conundrum.

Envision that you have taken on a legal case that turns out can be aided via the judicious use of an AI-based LegalTech app. In your capacity as a human lawyer, you run the AI app and it provides fortunately some handy insights about the underlying legal matters of the case. Great, the AI has been a useful tool for your adjudicative needs.

We are next going to make a big leap ahead of time, so please bear with me on this. At some time in the future, it is conceivable that there will be AI good enough to take on a legal case without the need for a human lawyer being involved. Instead, clients will make use of the autonomous form of AI that can handle a legal case from the proverbial A-to-Z aspects of the legal wrangling.

As an aside, some might argue that this notion is wholly farfetched and only something of a sci-fi kind of craziness. I guess it depends upon your viewpoint about the future. Suppose that this AI is designated for handling parking tickets? Or perhaps used for small claims court types of disputes? You see, the notion of the AI being able to handle legal matters does not necessarily suggest that the AI would be used in the most grandiose of legal settings. We might start small and eventually make our way to larger and more encompassing uses.

Anyway, we need to shift our attention to the legal goals and objectives considerations.

Some legal researchers have been wringing their hands that one of the presumed weaknesses or inherent limitations about AI in the law is that AI allegedly cannot set its own goals and objectives. AI is said to be devoid of the consciousness and sentience required to set goals and objectives. Only humans have this capacity and there is little expectation that anytime soon will we have the kind of AI that attains consciousness and sentience.

Before I tackle this bit of confounding logic, allow me to also indicate where the foundation for this assumption about AI is usually sourced from. The typical quote that is cited comes from a popular textbook on AI, and the selected quotation is this: "Because machines, unlike humans, have no objectives of their own, we give them objectives to achieve. In other words, we build optimizing machines, we feed objectives into them, and off they go" (per the textbook by Stuart Russell and Peter Norvig, *Artificial Intelligence: A Modern Approach*, 2021).

From this kind of quote, the logic of the rest of the argument about AI in the law as being inadequate regarding setting legal goals and objectives usually arises. The underpinning for the argument is based or seemingly bolstered due to the plucked indication of experts on AI regarding the believed limitations of AI concerning AI self-identifying goals and objectives.

As a side note, I've mentioned in other of my writings about AI-in-the-law that those legal researchers that conventionally are strong on their legal knowledge but weak on AI-background knowledge should be cautious in selecting or at times cherry-picking various proclamations or declarations about what AI is or is not. It would be akin to an AI steeped researcher cherry-picking some snippet about the law and trying to build the rest of their artifice on a potentially flimsy legal footing.

Nonetheless, the point by legal researchers taking this line of argument about legal goals and objectives is that if we had AI that was supposed to be your legal representative, handling a legal case for you akin to a human attorney, a potential glaring concern is that the AI won't be able to set its own legal goals and objectives. Thus, a human lawyer would be presumably a much better choice, else you'll be dealing with a legal adviser that notably lacks a capacity that a human attorney does have.

There are lots of questionably embedded considerations in that logic, which for brevity I'll just cover a few herein.

First, even the most ardently vocal of such legal researchers would concede that humans can presumably make goals and objectives *for* AI, either by directly programming the AI to have this or by otherwise guiding the AI accordingly. In that sense, one might counterargue that there is little significant difference that the AI itself cannot derive its own legal goals and objectives since we could merely program the AI or guide the AI as such. This then seems to dispense somewhat with the angst over the AI not being able to set its own legal goals and objectives (being instead handed to the AI).

Second, if you argue that the handing of legal goals and objectives to the AI is a cheat, namely that the AI ought to divine legal goals and objectives entirely on its own, I would ask you to consider how human lawyers derive legal goals and objectives. Do they do so out of thin air? Not really. They have likely been trained during law school or learned on-the-job about doing so. In that manner of speaking, you could assert that the human attorney is given or "handed" their legal goals and objectives, either by the actual version or via being trained how to derive them.

Third, we presumably could seek to train AI to try and establish its own legal goals and objectives. This might be handy so that we don't need to have a human lawyer by-hand compose them or even instruct the AI on what they are. Via various AI techniques and technologies, such as Machine Learning, it seems quite realistic to expect that we could program AI to relatively sufficiently self-identify legal goals and objectives for a given legal case (if sufficient and appropriately trained for this).

I think that provides a semblance of why the qualms about AI and legal goals and objectives are not necessarily as gloomy as they otherwise might seem on the surface.

Section 3: Conclusion

Before some of you jump out of your skin and exhort that I am suggesting AI will be sentient and exhibit consciousness, nothing I've said herein indicates such a contention.

Allow me to provide a quick analogous situation that might clarify what I am trying to say.

There are chess-playing AI-based systems today that can compete at the topmost levels of human players. Indeed, one might say that by and large the best of the AI chess-playing systems can eclipse even the best of the human players.

If you look closely at the AI systems used for this top-level chess playing, they usually have various embedded chess-oriented goals and objectives. There are overarching goals and subordinated goals. There are overarching objectives and subordinated objectives. Throughout a chess match, various goals and objectives are tracked, along with adjustments made as to which goals and objectives continue to make the most sense given the status of the game midway through.

There is nothing about that kind of AI that smacks of consciousness and nor sentience. My assertion is that we can consider the handling of legal cases in a somewhat comparable way to chess-playing (well, obviously, there are a lot of crucial differences, since chess is not open-ended, etc.). An AI system could be programmed with legal goals and objectives, or be programmed to derive them or be trained to derive them, and so on. This is without any iota of AI consciousness or sentience.

That all being said, I am wholeheartedly in agreement that one of the limitations for AI as we know it today is that it lacks consciousness and sentience. And that this absence of such an earthshattering capacity is a huge limiter as to what we can expect today's AI to be able to undertake. No doubts about that.

I would also patently agree that having today's AI take on legal cases on its own accord is rife with problems and generally ill-advised and impractical. The open question is whether advances in AI techniques and technologies will allow us to move in that direction, or whether we will need consciousness and sentience in AI to get there.

If your headstrong definition of being able to set goals and objectives is that only that which has consciousness and sentience can do so, then indeed by that claimed definition there is currently zero chance of today's AI setting goals and objectives. Do we though need to make inseparable the act of setting goals and objectives as being only done by that which has consciousness and sentience?

Note: *For supplemental materials depicting the aspects discussed in this chapter, refer to Appendix B, which contains various augmented diagrams, charts, and additional related facets of relevance.*

CHAPTER 20

AI & LAW: OXFORD DEBATE AI VERSUS AI

Key briefing points about this essay:

- AI in the law is rising as an important professional realm for the legal profession
- Meanwhile, there is a parallel growth in the study of and need for AI ethics
- Oxford Union Society recently held a debate about AI ethics
- Some controversy was that the debate occurred by AI pitted against AI
- Many insights for AI-in-the-law can be gleaned from the matter

Section 1: Introduction

I dare say that most lawyers relish a good debate.

This notion of savoring any especially outstanding debates would seem rooted in the importance of legal argumentation as a crucial element of practicing law. Attorneys are called upon to craft legal arguments. Those legal arguments are supposed to be notably robust and ironclad strong.

The fate of your client and your legal case depends upon your ability to create and convey a suitably legally-convincing argument.

As such, there is a chance of learning something new or advantageous when witnessing a tightly woven debate of nearly any kind, even when the debate might have nothing seemingly to do with the law. The very aspect that a debate entails vociferous argumentation is sufficiently vital to be able to glean morsels of how to better construct your own legal arguments. A generic argument can often be transposed into instructive means of deriving legal arguments.

All this talk about debates is due to a recent debate that was undertaken by the famous Oxford Union Society, known globally as a premier debating organization (and, by the way, a separate entity apart from Oxford University). Since being founded in 1823, this venerated group has hosted some of the most noteworthy debates in history. Renowned debaters during this storied time period have often included highly influential experts across all walks of society, encompassing politics, science, culture, etc.

Their recent headline-grabbing debate was performed in conjunction with Oxford's Said Business School and was an outcrop of a post-graduate class studying AI. The topic of the debate centered on the ethics of high-tech and generally pontificated on whether AI might become too powerful for mankind to handle.

The topic of AI ethics has been gaining a lot of attention lately.

Whereas the initial belief was that *AI For Good* would be the sole means of utilizing AI, many have come to realize that there is also the *AI For Bad* that presents great challenges too. Studies have shown that some AI systems were derived based on data that was inherently biased or contained inequities, which in turn the trained AI system then incorporated.

In short, there are lots of ways that AI is going to proffer sour outcomes and we need to be on the watch accordingly.

This brings us to the doorstep of AI in the law.

You see, there are two major ways to intertwine AI and the law: (1) AI as applied to the law and the practice of law, (2) Law as applied to the advent of AI.

In the first case, lawyers and legal scholars emphasize the use of AI as applied to the law, which I'll signify as the so-called robo-lawyer, robo-judge, robo-juror, and the like kinds of aspirations. Note that I am not a fan of that robo verbiage, but it is admittedly a quick way to invoke the imagery of what applied AI is ultimately aiming to do.

In the second case, the focus is on how to best establish laws to ensure the appropriate regulation and governance over AI. This is considered using or leveraging the law as applied to AI.

Section 2: Lessons About AI In The Law As Uncovered Via The Debate

Now that we've set the stage for our discussion, let's jump into the reasons that this Oxford Union debate has some demonstrative value for those interested in the matter of AI-in-the-law.

Get ready for a bit of a surprise. I earlier left out the most outwardly startling element about the debate, indeed the primary basis for why it garnered outsized headlines, namely that the debate had AI debating against AI. Yes, as odd as it might seem, this was not a traditional human-to-human debate but instead a provocative AI-to-AI debate.

Via the help of some outside tech vendors that specialize in AI, the debate was put together such that one AI-based computer system was debating with another AI-based computer system. The AI systems were devised to vocalize the debate so that audience members could hear what was going on (akin to an Alexa or Siri vocalization).

All of the AI was shaped around a prior given debate question that was stated as: "This house believes that AI will never be ethical."

One of the AI systems was programmed to argue that AI will never be ethically compromised per se since it is only a machine and presumably devoid of innate ethical considerations. The other AI system was programmed to counterargue that AI will inevitably be embedded into human brains and ergo will be intermixed with the already ethical dilemmas of mankind.

This considered "stunt" of using AI in this debating scheme has given rise to many untoward issues and outright qualms about this rather "rigged" debate. I'll try to cover some of the key concerns and remain relatively brief. Nonetheless, please know that the debate has been characterized as rubbing the wrong way some of those that revere the debating organization, exhorting that this was a "sell-out" of their core principles, in a manner of speaking.

The co-director of the course and that was avidly a producer of the debate was reported as admitting that the debate could be characterized as a type of gimmick.

One supposes that it is feasible to stand tall and insist that any debate that draws attention to the rising challenges and threats from AI would be of meritorious value. On the other hand, the debate format and approach could be said to detract from an altogether serious and somber topic, essentially backfiring by making a mockery of the debate topic per se.

You'll have to decide which side of that acrimonious view you wish to reside on.

Anyway, a first key point of essential clarification is that the AI was programmed by humans to say what it said. This is important to realize. Sadly, we continue to see in the mass media an illusory sense that AI has reached a level of consciousness and sentience as though it can think by its own volition. This is absolutely not the case. Unfortunately, stunts that showcase AI doing things as though it has achieved human levels of reasoning are an outstretched form of anthropomorphizing of AI.

This gives society a false impression of what today's AI can do, setting misimpressions that are hard to undo. Furthermore, egregiously, when the falsehood is perpetrated as part of a well-known and otherwise considered noble organization, one can suggest that it makes such tomfoolery even worse.

Secondly, the depth of the arguments made, and the width of the arguments on this stridently vital topic about AI and ethics was ostensibly quite disappointing and shallow. Whether this was due to a preoccupied focus on making the AI work for the debate or maybe due to a lack of awareness by those crafting the underlying high-tech regarding what the debate fully entails, the result, in any case, was that the debate turned out in the eyes of some experts on this topic as a sorely sloppy one and lacking in vigor.

If you are going to have a debate on AI ethics, and especially by a top-notch debating organization, the hope was that the debate would be entirely comprehensive and invigorating. The question then becomes whether the gimmickry overshadowed the content and complexity of the warranted debate.

Returning to the aspect of how this all connects with AI in the law, we can quickly glean some insightful lessons.

When crafting legal arguments, one would presumably attend to the substance of the argument. In addition, some lawyers and legal researchers acknowledge that at times the gimmickry surrounding a legal argument can be an equally important consideration. Legal arguments are seen as a form of legal storytelling, and the means to get juries for example to be swayed by a legal argument can consist of using relevant puffery or embellishment as might seem suitable (within bounds).

If we are going to have AI systems that aid attorneys in crafting legal arguments, should the AI also advise on or even create embellishments for the human lawyer to consider using?

Some say this is plainly wrong, others say it is plainly practical and aboveboard.

At some future point, assuming that AI robo-lawyering becomes feasible and AI acts autonomously in a legal advisory manner, should such AI make use of embellishments as part of legal arguments?

Again, some say this is plainly wrong, others say it is plainly practical and aboveboard (all's fair in love and war, they might contend).

Shifting direction, another lesson from the debate is that the ethical behavior of AI is going to need to be overtly laid out and that we are undoubtedly going to require laws that provide guidance covering how AI should be designed, built, fielded, and maintained to be considered both lawful and ethically proper.

Lawyers specializing in AI-in-the-law will be of special merit for working with lawmakers to devise such laws. In addition, attorneys versed in AI-in-the-law will likely be needed by clients that have promulgated AI systems that have seemingly gone beyond the lawful parameters, getting the human developers into legal hot waters.

There is a fundamental duality that encompasses AI ethics and AI in the law.

Section 3: Conclusion

One last point for now.

Attorneys and jurists need to know that the AI of today is not sentient. There are so many false or misleading claims about AI sentience that it could readily cause some lawyers and some judges to become confused about what AI can attain. That's not good.

I trust that by herein discussing the recent debate, you are now more solidly aware that AI is not sentient, but that's only due to your having gone beyond the headline-grabbing astonishments.

Good for you and please pass along the word to your fellow practitioners of the law).

Note: *For supplemental materials depicting the aspects discussed in this chapter, refer to Appendix B, which contains various augmented diagrams, charts, and additional related facets of relevance.*

CHAPTER 21
AI & LAW:
ROUTINE LEGAL WORK

Key briefing points about this essay:

- AI in the law is gaining speed and increasingly being applied to many legal uses
- Usual ways of applying AI include e-Discovery, doing legal contracts analyses, etc.
- There are also AI-infused legal tools gradually being made available to consumers
- Most of this is typically shaped around so-called "legally routine tasks"
- This gives rise to exploring what is legally routine versus that which is non-routine

Section 1: Introduction

Some lawyers contend that they are going bonkers when doing routine legal work.

According to recent nationwide surveys, nearly two-thirds of professional workers reportedly indicated that they are tired of doing routine tasks and that the adverse effects include a precipitous drop in employee morale (the survey respondents included legal professionals).

One assumes that the decrease in morale translates into less interest in the job, poorer performance on the job, and can produce heightened turnover as workers seek other opportunities that are more inspiring.

For lawyers, the types of routine tasks notably bordering on tedium entail everyday types of court filings and other perceived legal grunt work. The consumption of "lawyering" labor for such legal services is certainly eyebrow-raising as to expending highly trained and highly-priced lawyering talent to undertake tasks that would seem viably done by less costly labor. Of course, law firms with suitable sizes are usually steeped with para-legal professionals and other such staff to try and take on the routine tasks that do not especially require attorney-level acumen.

It might at first glance seem obvious as to how to ascertain that a legal task can be classified as being routine. Let's dig into that assumed notion.

Imagine assembling a collection of legal artifacts into one comprehensive set for purposes of distribution to other parties of a legal case.

Is this a legal task that is routine or non-routine?

On the one hand, you could claim that the task is routine if there was no semblance of legal acuity required to perform the task. If this was simply the tedious chore of collecting the needed artifacts, perhaps scanning some in for machine readability, and then accumulating them into one electronic-based digital document, presumably the amount of legal acumen needed is minimal (or zero).

Suppose though that the choice of which artifacts to include required attorney-level legal reasoning. And that the sequencing of the documents likewise required astute legal reasoning. Etc. Does this now push the boundaries of seemingly routine work into non-routine legal work?

While you ponder that pickle, consider a more pronounced example.

Some would readily assert that drafting a legal document and reviewing a legal document such as a contract is ostensibly not routine work. For this, certainly, you need to exercise keen legal reasoning and leverage the capacities of a lawyer.

As you likely are aware, there are online programs that nowadays perform some semblance of legal document preparation and review, as mentioned by this legal researcher: "In the past, Americans who wanted to handle their own routine needs without a lawyer might have tried to buy a book of forms or consulted a form-processing service with limited ability to provide customized assistance. Now those customers can meet their legal needs with LegalZoom or Rocket Lawyer, frequently at a price that no attorney can afford to match" (by authors Benjamin Barton and Deborah Rhode, "Access To Justice and Routine Legal Services: New Technologies Meet Bar Regulators" in *Hastings Law Journal*, 2019).

If a computer can be used to undertake such a task, does this ergo imply that the task must indeed be of a legally routine caliber?

Some lawyers vehemently argue that those online programs are in fact performing legal services, routine or otherwise. The nature of what is legally routine has somewhat ill-defined connotations and will increasingly be a tough nut to crack. For those that believe these online programs are crossing over into the legal lawyering realm, the odds are that a strident argument will be made that these are decidedly not legally routine efforts. This in turn opens the door to shutting down those online programs by asserting that they violate key legal precepts concerning the practice of law.

To date, these online services have clung to the insistence that they are below such a threshold: "They do not, and under bar ethics rules and statutory prohibitions, cannot offer services that constitute the practice of law. Their disclaimers make clear that they are, as LegalZoom notes in bold on its platform, 'not acting as your attorney,' and 'not a substitute for the advice of an attorney.' Rocket Lawyer similarly declares it does not provide legal advice, but only a platform for legal information and self-help" (per the article by Barton and Rhode).

There is yet another perspective on what constitutes legally routine work.

An attorney that day in and day out creates roughly the same legal contracts for various clients, all contracts of which are almost identical would probably lean toward stating that they are being underutilized in a legally routine manner (even if there were genuine legal insights required to perform the task at hand).

In short, there would seem to be at least these facets of legally routine work:

1) Transparent Routine – legal work involving no bona fide semblance of legal acumen
2) Base Routine – legal work requiring legally minimal legal acumen
3) Upscale Routine - requiring legal reasoning but repetitively and with little added value
4) Non-Routine – legal work that is reasonably said to require devout legal acumen

Admittedly, there is room for debate related to the definitiveness of each category. Without more stringent metrics, arguments could be made as to where each one begins and ends. We'll put that aside for the moment and proceed with the discussion since the focus is on a different angle about this all-told topic.

Shifting gears, AI is stepping up the game of using automation for performing legal tasks.

You likely already know about especially popular ways of applying AI in the law such as infusing Natural Language Processing (NLP) capabilities into the arduous chore of doing e-Discovery (i.e., AI-based NLP is especially useful when dealing with large-scale narrative-oriented datasets that require extensive and otherwise laborious by-hand legal discovery efforts). And you are perhaps familiar with the use of AI for aiding in examining and composing legal contracts.

The list of such AI-applied uses is continually growing.

Please also know that there are two major ways to intertwine AI and the law: (1) AI as applied to the law and the practice of law, (2) Law as applied to the advent of AI. In the first case, which is the focus of this discussion, lawyers and legal scholars emphasize the use of AI as applied to the law, which I'll signify as the so-called robo-lawyer, robo-judge, robo-juror, and the like kinds of aspirations. Note that I am not a fan of that robo verbiage, but it is admittedly a quick way to invoke the imagery of what applied AI is ultimately aiming to do.

Section 2: Exploring The Opposing Camps On AI And Legal Routine Work

Now that we've set the stage for our discussion, let's jump into the conundrum about routine legal tasks.

One use of AI as applied to performing legal tasks consists of lawyers using such high-tech tools. In that sense, the AI is somewhat hidden from clients and merely part and parcel of an attorney undertaking their legal tasks, perhaps akin to using a word processing package or using a spreadsheet package to get their work done.

Another use of AI in the law consists of making AI-based lawyering tools available to non-lawyers such as consumers (which might otherwise be construed as prospective clients for human attorneys). This is already underway: "Some see a future in which legal artificial intelligence ('AI') will largely replace humans in providing legal advice and drafting documents.

Others doubt that AI will progress that far. But, everyone agrees that computers are already displacing human lawyers in areas like document review and assembly and will likely continue to do so" (per Barton and Rhode).

You could argue that the AI usage for consumers is only targeting the "routine" legal work and therefore not a particularly unsettling encroachment on attorneys.

Indeed, tying back to the earlier points about attorneys potentially being dissatisfied with having to perform routine work, perhaps AI capabilities solves that dilemma. Clients would take on the routine work themselves via the leveraging of AI. After which, they presumably would come to human attorneys solely for non-routine work that truly invokes legal acumen (and no longer bother them with routine work).

Meanwhile, you might argue that the clients ought to still bring the routine work to the human attorneys, doing so under the presumption that lawyers will use AI as part of their lawyering efforts to undertake any routine legal tasks. Thus, the attorney uses the AI and presumably can reduce their labor efforts (and costs) accordingly, parceling out the routine legal tasks to (one assumes) less costly AI-based legal-focused tools.

As the famous line in the classic movie *The Princess Bride* suggests, this whole can of worms is only just getting started to be opened.

One concern is that attorneys relying upon the AI to do their legally routine tasks will gradually and inexorably become deskilled at being a lawyer. The slippery slope here is that by no longer undertaking the routine legal tasks, this undercuts the lawyer's ability to perform the non-routine legal tasks (i.e., the routine and the non-routine are ultimately exercising the same "legal muscles" as it were).

Here's yet another qualm.

If AI can chew away at legally routine tasks, suppose this eventually becomes commonly viable and nothing is remaining for AI to tackle in the routine legal task milieu. It would seem patently obvious that the AI would be extended to try and perform non-routine legal work. This then presumably threatens lawyers as to displace them in a much more substantive way than does the crunching of routine legal work.

We can turn this somewhat on its head too.

Some would argue that if we don't seek to apply AI to the non-routine legal tasks, we are going to undercut what AI can potentially attain for us as a society. By somehow apriori deciding that the AI should only be used for routine legal tasks, we will limit the range and depth of benefits that advanced AI can provide. We have either wasted AI or have prelimited how far we are aiming to extend AI (shortened the goalposts, one might say).

Section 3: Conclusion

Returning to the postulated levels of legally routine tasks (which included the fourth category, non-routine too, for sake of completeness), the odds would seem in favor of AI developers snaking their way toward applying AI into the law by proceeding from Stage 1 and making their way until they get to Stage 4.

Of some relief to today's attorneys is that we are still grappling with the stages less than the fourth one, therefore there is a temporary reprieve before the non-routine legal work is bound to be AI-infused.

For those that worry that the whole procession is worrisome and that none of the stages should be amendable to using AI, you ought to not be overly smug since the march of progress in AI is gunning for those legal activities.

Note: *For supplemental materials depicting the aspects discussed in this chapter, refer to Appendix B, which contains various augmented diagrams, charts, and additional related facets of relevance.*

CHAPTER 22

AI & LAW: BANDWAGON NETWORK EFFECT

Key briefing points about this article:

- AI in the law is gaining speed and increasingly being applied to many legal uses
- Usual ways of applying AI include e-Discovery, doing legal contracts analyses, etc.
- There are also AI-infused legal tools gradually being made available to consumers
- Some claim that whoever is first will catch hold of the marketplace
- We explore whether this bandwagon network effect will arise in AI-in-the-law

Section 1: Introduction

How did Facebook become so immensely dominant in social media?

Unless you have been living under a rock or inside a cave, you certainly must already realize the enormity of Facebook. Recent estimates indicate that there are nearly 3 billion monthly active users on Facebook. That is a quite staggering number.

Some insist that Facebook has become a monopoly and that we need a strong dose of antitrust to curtail the fearsome Facebook juggernaut. Of course, Facebook doesn't see things that way. They vehemently argue that there is plenty of competition in the social media realm. People can readily choose to use Facebook, and likewise can readily choose to not use Facebook. Nobody is being forced into becoming a Facebook user, they indignantly emphasize. Use someone else's platform, if you so prefer.

We ought to at least acknowledge the amazing feat of Facebook in terms of having attained such unimaginable popularity, and marvel at the accomplishment thereof. Returning to my initial opening question for this discussion, what magic potion or hypnotic spell did Facebook use to garner the colossal userbase that it enjoys today?

Simply stated, you can attribute the eye-opening growth to the now-classic *bandwagon network effect.*

Here's the way that a bandwagon network effect works. You get some people to initially start using your service or product. The perceived value of the service or product is that the more users there are, the better it is to be a member or subscriber, or purchaser. Thus, those that have already chosen to use the service or product are apt to reach out to others and urge them to join too.

Eventually, human nature takes over and FOMO (fear of missing out) sparks others to join, regardless of whether anyone specifically asked them to do so. As they say, you never want to be the last one to arrive at a party. So, soon enough, two people spur two more, and those two more each spur two more, and the next thing you know there is this cascading nearly exponential growth pattern.

Notice something else that is crucial in this fascinating phenomenon. Whichever such platform seems to be growing fastest and ostensibly is the largest (or perceived as most popular) is bound to get all the spoils. People decide that is the "right one" to join. A kind of magnetic attraction occurs. Even if there are competing platforms, they can be left in the dust as the spiraling gravitational sense of user magnitude dovetails toward pulling in more people as though by an invisible hand.

Voila, the bandwagon network effect.

People join the bandwagon. The bandwagon thrives off of networking. This effect repeats and repeats, reaching grand peaks.

Meanwhile, other competing platforms might find themselves up a creek without a paddle. No matter what they do, they are not able to replicate the same effect. Sure, they might be growing and doing so with an impressive rate, but the odds are they won't strike gold in the same manner as the other player that has by luck or skill found themselves immersed in the bandwagon network effect.

The bandwagon network effect can potentially wear off. I mention this because the underlying platform cannot necessarily rest on its laurels. Despite the stickiness of having such a dominant presence and volume of users, there is always the chance that the bandwagon subsides. You've got to keep your bandwagon going else it will likely inexorably deplete and something else might rise to take your place.

You might be vaguely aware that the Silicon Valley high-tech community has an indelibly inscribed mantra about always trying to be first, which ties into this bandwagon milieu. The logic is that if you are the first to get a new kind of service or product into the marketplace, you will latch onto the bandwagon network effect and speed past any follow-along competitors.

This is somewhat of a myth of sorts since it isn't guaranteed that the first will get the bandwagon. But, anyway, being first can be advantageous at times (and can also have its decided disadvantages too).

Why have I dragged you through this engaging discussion about the venerated bandwagon network effect?

Because some believe that the same phenomenon is going to happen in the legal field, specifically related to the emergence of AI in the law.

I'd like to unpack the claim and walk you through the merits and shortcomings of the asserted notion. Before we can get into the meat of things, it would be handy to make sure we are all on the same page about the matter of AI-in-the-law.

AI is stepping up the game of using automation for performing legal tasks, oftentimes being an added capability on top of some other "conventional" computer-based LegalTech app or system. You likely already know about especially popular ways of applying AI in the law such as infusing Natural Language Processing (NLP) capabilities into the arduous chore of doing e-Discovery (i.e., AI-based NLP is especially useful when dealing with large-scale narrative-oriented datasets that require extensive and otherwise laborious by-hand legal discovery efforts). And you are perhaps familiar with the use of AI for aiding in examining and composing legal contracts.

The list of such AI-applied uses is continually growing.

Please also know that there are two major ways to intertwine AI and the law: (1) AI as applied to the law and the practice of law, (2) Law as applied to the advent of AI. In the first case, which is the focus of this discussion, lawyers and legal scholars emphasize the use of AI as applied to the law, which I'll signify as the so-called robo-lawyer, robo-judge, robo-juror, and the like kinds of aspirations. Note that I am not a fan of that robo verbiage, but it is admittedly a quick way to invoke the imagery of what applied AI is ultimately aiming to do.

Section 2: Exploring The Bandwagon Network Effect For AI In The Law

Now that I've set the stage properly, we can jump into the contentions surrounding a bandwagon network effect as it applies to the advent of AI in the law.

In particular, the presumption is that whoever first attains some niche in the AI-in-the-law realm, will ergo also enjoy the rewards of the bandwagon network effect. For example, if a vendor comes out with the knock-your-socks-off AI for doing contracts analyses and formulation, and does so first, lawyers will come running to buy or subscribe to it. This in turn will spur other lawyers to buy or subscribe to it.

The bandwagon network effect will turn it into a dazzling star.

Legal researchers suggest that LegalZoom and Rocket Lawyer have experienced this kind of growth, though of course aiming not at legal professionals per se and instead of seeking to enable consumers as non-lawyers to undertake what might arguably be considered legal-related tasks. Here's how authors Benjamin Barton and Deborah Rhode describe this: "In these markets, individuals generally prefer to go to the one site that everyone uses because as more people use the service, the service actually improves. Network effects make the competition in emerging information markets particularly fierce because often there will be only one survivor. This is one of the central drivers of the 'winner-take-all' economy. The victor will also reap monopoly profits, which further increases the stakes. Add all of these factors together and you have a pretty rough and tumble battle for market dominance" (by authors Benjamin Barton and Deborah Rhode, "Access To Justice and Routine Legal Services: New Technologies Meet Bar Regulators" in Hastings Law Journal, 2019).

This gives me a moment to comment on the multitude of directions associated with AI-in-the-law when it comes to applying AI to performing legal tasks.

One aim would be to arm lawyers with AI-based legal aiding tools. The lawyer is still in-charge and a tool is merely a tool.

Another angle is to craft AI-based legal tools that are relatively autonomous. This means that a human lawyer is not required. The AI itself can perform seemingly legal-oriented tasks. As an aside, this is something that is going to raise all heck amongst the legal community and the ever-present UPL (unauthorized practice of law) provisions.

For AI-based legal tools of an autonomous nature, the thinking is that consumers or non-lawyers will be able to use such tools in lieu of consulting a human attorney.

You'll see in a moment why I bring up those several paths.

Section 3: Conclusion

The deal is that some claim we will witness a bandwagon network effect within those paths.

You see, the first vendor to devise a consumer-oriented AI-based legal tool that autonomously will handle your divorce from A to Z, well, the assumption is that this will grab the market by the shirt collar and skyrocket due to the bandwagon network effect.

Likewise, the first vendor to devise a lawyer-using AI-based legal tool to craft bona fide legal arguments will find themselves being besieged by attorneys desirous of buying or subscribing. In turn, this will expand and explode into a grand network effect.

Do you believe that this winner-take-all will indeed occur in the AI-in-the-law arena?

Overall, it seems a bit optimistic, perhaps dreamy-eyed. There is assuredly a first-mover advantage that can occur, and we ought to not overlook or understate that uplifting potential. At the same time, being first when you don't have the right stuff, can savagely undercut the bandwagon network effect.

Some would even argue that you can cut your own throat by being first. The first AI product out the gate might be so flawed and inept that the vendor and the product or service become forever branded as unworthy. Even if you, later on, overcome the flaws, the stigma might remain attached, and the bandwagon gets muddled with old smears and buckets of mud.

All of that being the case, there is still excitement about being first. I don't want to discourage those courageous enough to break new ground. I will also say that those coming along behind the first mover should not toss in the towel. You might be the one that has the magic touch and manages to be the winner of the bandwagon network effect.

Note: *For supplemental materials depicting the aspects discussed in this chapter, refer to Appendix B, which contains various augmented diagrams, charts, and additional related facets of relevance.*

CHAPTER 23

AI & LAW: THEORY VERSUS PRACTICE

Key briefing points about this essay:

- AI in the law is gaining speed and increasingly being applied to many legal uses
- Usual ways of applying AI include e-Discovery, doing legal contracts analyses, etc.
- Some though proclaim that we are hitting a wall on progress for AI-in-the-law
- Focus instead on crafting new theories, set aside that primal urge to build
- All told, this is commonly couched as though one side or the other can only prevail

Section 1: Introduction

There are two sides to every coin.

That being said, it is still one coin.

I'll come back to that seemingly sage wisdom in a moment.

Amidst those focused on advancing the use of AI in the law, there is an ongoing and at times acrimonious debate about the value of theory versus the utility of putting something into practice or use. Some insist that the only viable means of truly making significant advances will arise by extending and devising new theories underlying AI in the law. Others counterargue that the theory approach will not get us any semblance of traction, such that the only real proof of the pudding will be to build and attempt to actively use real-world AI-in-the-law apps and systems.

Yes, this is the classic theory-versus-practice debate that has preoccupied attention in nearly every domain or academic discipline since the beginning of human thought (well, that might be a bit overstated, but you get the gist, I assume).

Do you think that our best and brightest hope of making large leaping-sized strides in AI-in-the-law will come from innovative theories, or will it come due to trying to put AI high-tech into the throes and morass of day-to-day legal endeavors?

Before you answer that question (though you might already have a predilection in mind), let's back up and make sure we are all on the same page about AI-in-the-law.

You likely know that AI is stepping up the game of using automation for performing legal tasks, oftentimes being an added capability on top of some other "conventional" computer-based LegalTech app or system. Especially popular ways of applying AI in the law consist of infusing Natural Language Processing (NLP) capabilities into the arduous chore of doing e-Discovery (i.e., AI-based NLP is especially useful when dealing with large-scale narrative-oriented datasets that require extensive and otherwise laborious by-hand legal discovery efforts). And you are perhaps familiar with the use of AI for aiding in examining and composing legal contracts.

The list of such AI-applied uses is continually growing.

Please also know that there are two major ways to intertwine AI and the law: (1) AI as applied to the law and the practice of law, (2) Law as applied to the advent of AI. In the first case, which is the focus of this discussion, lawyers and legal scholars emphasize the use of AI as applied to the law, which I'll signify as the so-called robo-lawyer, robo-judge, robo-juror, and the like kinds of aspirations. Note that I am not a fan of that robo verbiage, but it is admittedly a quick way to invoke the imagery of what applied AI is ultimately aiming to do.

Section 2: Two Sides Butting Heads

There aren't any robo-lawyers or robo-jurists as yet, despite whatever snazzy eye-candy headlines might loudly proclaim. We are a long distance from that anticipated future. Furthermore, as added clarification, there isn't any AI today that is sentient. That too is a headline-grabbing claim that seems to be popping up, namely that someone declares they crafted AI that is sentient. Don't believe it.

We don't know if we can craft or generate that kind of AI. Nor can we say when it will occur if it in fact is able to someday be achieved.

Right now, within the AI-in-the-law context, the primary aim entails arming lawyers with AI-based legal aiding tools. The lawyer is still in-charge and a tool is merely a tool. Another angle is to eventually craft AI-based legal tools that are relatively autonomous. This means that a human lawyer is not required to perform the scoped legal tasks. The AI itself can perform seemingly legal-oriented tasks. As an aside, this is something that is going to raise thorny issues amongst the legal community and the ever-present UPL (unauthorized practice of law) provisions.

The bottom-line consideration herein is that we are still in the infancy of AI-in-the-law. Baby steps are taking place. Some even assert that we are already at a kind of wall, stunted in terms of getting AI-in-the-law closer to the autonomous dream.

What is holding us back?

Not good enough theories assert one camp. Put aside the eager desire to build AI-in-the-law machinery and instead aid in deriving better theories. Those theories might be in AI. Those theories might be about the law. And those theories might be about the intersection of AI and the law. In any case, robust and outstanding theories will get us beyond today's roadblocks.

You are missing the mark, contends the counterargument, it isn't more theories that we need, but instead, we need more applied and practical AI-in-the-law systems. For each such system so constructed, we are inching our way forward. Those conceptual theories are nice, perhaps heartwarming, yet they do little to deal with the complexities and problems that are only solved when the AI rubbers meet the road, so to speak. Build, build, build. The theories can either catch up or merely be a thing of astounding abstract beauty that looks good and makes for rather lofty discussions.

Wait for a second, some retort to these acrid debaters, why can't we do both at the same time?

This seems like a sound path. Do some theory, test it by building an AI-in-the-law system. Based on the testing and fielding, loop back to the underlying theories. Revamp those theories as needed. Thus, make a theory, put it into practice, and then rinse and repeat.

Surely, this would glean us the best of both worlds.

Section 3: Conclusion

Believe it or not, such an ostensibly fair and balanced proposed means of advancing AI-in-the-law is often rejected by *both sides* of the coin.

The theory side emphasizes that the builders are apt to misconstrue the theories and inadequately construct an AI-in-the-law system. If the relevant AI-in-the-law system falters, the theory will take the blame, unfairly so. In turn, the theory might get blackballed or otherwise sourly tainted.

The practice side exhorts that trying to apply some of these theories is crazy because we need more tools and practical uses to figure out how to implement them. Let's keep our eyes on the ball and stridently pursue the implementation aspects. Dealing with theories is energy-draining and unworthy.

In short, the argument about the theory-versus-practice is often stated as a zero-sum gambit. For each iota of attention to theory, you are ripping off an iota that could have gone toward an implementation. Likewise, for each iota toward building something, you are denying an iota that could have fruitfully gone toward the emergence of new theories.

For those that ask for both sides to coexist and multiply each other, the reply is that you can't do that. You must choose one side or the other. Join one camp. You can't be in both camps. Zero-sum is the key winner that overrides any chance of doing both.

What do you think?

One coin, two sides, and the matter of which gets the preference is still being debated. Solemnly, you can at least be assured that this is an enduring debate that will persist for a long time to come.

Note: *For supplemental materials depicting the aspects discussed in this chapter, refer to Appendix B, which contains various augmented diagrams, charts, and additional related facets of relevance.*

CHAPTER 24
AI & LAW: LAW SCHOOLS VERSUS COMPUTER SCIENCE

Key briefing points about this essay:

- AI in the law is gaining speed and increasingly being applied to many legal uses
- Usual ways of applying AI include e-Discovery, doing legal contracts analyses, etc.
- There is also the application of the law to AI, aiming to regulate AI accordingly
- Academics sitting squarely in AI-in-the-law are often faced with a tough choice
- You can reside in a law school, or computer science, though not without controversy

Section 1: Introduction

If AI and the law are like two peas in a pod, where should that pod reside?

This is actually a quite sobering and seriously pursued question. In case you weren't already aware of the ongoing conundrum, there is a polite and yet at times acrimonious debate about where the academic field of AI-in-the-law should reside.

First, as a point of clarification, almost no one would ostensibly argue that AI-in-the-law is not altogether an interdisciplinary realm, which seems obvious on the face of things. You've got the AI side of the matter. You've got the law or legal domain side of the matter. Joining the two together gets you into the AI-in-the-law intersecting sphere.

It would seem a bit odd to contend that AI-in-the-law is solely confined within the field of law. Likewise, it would seem a bit peculiar to claim that AI-in-the-law is exclusively in the AI field. You have to freely admit that it is a twofer. They are intertwined and there is no getting around that stark fact.

Okay, since we seem to be reasonably agreeable to the notion that AI-in-the-law is two things at once, unfortunately, this does not solve the enduring dilemma that has gone on for ages and will undoubtedly remain contentious. Allow me to directly point out the thorny issue.

The sharped-edged question is this: Should AI-in-the-law as an academic discipline be placed in law schools, or should it be housed in computer science departments (wherein the study of AI usually resides)?

One ardent viewpoint is that AI-in-the-law rightfully and unquestionably belongs in law schools. The law side of the topic is the ruling king, as it were. Ergo, the whole shebang ought to be comfortably snug and ensconced into law schools.

Whoa, exhort those that take the contrasting perspective, the AI is what makes AI-in-the-law summarily of keen interest and worthy of effusive attention. Let's make sure that we properly acknowledge that the AI is the shining beacon and therefore the veritable kit and caboodle needs to be in computer science. The law part is merely an offshoot of how AI can be applied to a myriad of domains, such as the legal domain, the medical domain, the financial domain, and the like.

Before we dig further into this debate and discourse, I'd like to straighten out what it means to refer to AI-in-the-law. I say this because many are often taking a lopsided or narrow view of what the realm consists of.

Please know that there are two major ways to intertwine AI and the law: (1) AI as applied to the law and the practice of law, (2) Law as applied to the advent of AI.

In the first instance, lawyers and legal scholars emphasize the use of AI as applied to the law, which I'll signify as the so-called robo-lawyer, robo-judge, robo-juror, and the like kinds of aspirations. Note that I am not a fan of that robo verbiage, but it is admittedly a quick way to invoke the imagery of what applied AI is ultimately aiming to do.

The second instance consists of applying the law to AI, such as ascertaining how our laws and regulations should be adjusted or crafted anew to cope with the burgeoning use of AI throughout society. This is construed as using legal acumen to figure out the appropriate means of governing AI.

Let's noodle on this for a brief moment.

Much of the flashy aspects about AI-in-the-law stems from the application of AI into the law (that's the first case indicated above). Especially popular ways of applying AI in the law consist of infusing Natural Language Processing (NLP) capabilities into the arduous chore of doing e-Discovery (i.e., AI-based NLP is especially useful when dealing with large-scale narrative-oriented datasets that require extensive and otherwise laborious by-hand legal discovery efforts). And you are perhaps familiar with the use of AI for aiding in examining and composing legal contracts. There are lots of these infusions taking place of plopping AI techniques and technologies into the carrying out bona fide legal tasks.

I'd almost bet that you were probably thinking of AI-in-the-law as purely the application of AI to the law.

Time to expand that way of thinking.

Get ready for the next boon, namely the need to apply the law to AI. This is gradually gaining notable ground and outstretched headlines. Why so? This is partially due to the rampant and uncontrolled promulgating of AI that has showcased seedy and untoward capacities. The recent era of AI began with a rousing cheer that AI would be abundantly good for society, but quickly discovered that there is the grimy underbelly of AI too. AI systems are now suspect right away, often embedding contemptible biases in factors such as race, gender, etc. As a result, the applying of the law to AI is garnering a lot of steam.

Section 2: No Place To Call Home

You could make the case that the application of AI to the law is perhaps leaning more so on the AI aspects and somewhat less so on the legal aspects. The logic is that you have to know how to build and utilize AI, whereas the legal field is merely a domain upon which this takes place. Anybody that knows AI ought to be able to jump into the fray, it is so claimed.

Wrong, the retort goes.

If you want AI to properly perform legal tasks, you need to be just as deep into the law and legal intricacies as you do on the AI side. In fact, one common refrain is that AI embedded into the legal field has been stymied so far because the AI researchers arrogantly assumed that the law was a piece of cake. By being overstepped in AI, and under stepped in the law, presumably, they were not able to hit the mark.

That is the usual ramblings about AI applied to the law.

What about the akin rhetoric regarding the law as applied to AI?

As you might guess, the conventional wisdom has been that you need to really know the law, but you don't need to be as strongly versed in AI. All you need to do is construe AI as simply nothing more than some high-tech stuff. Just take whatever laws we have and readjust them for this newer kind of high-tech contrivance.

Others would disagree with that sentiment. They would argue that those versed in the law are at times confounding the situation by oversimplifying what AI is. Furthermore, those that don't know the realities of today's AI are likely to have the wool pulled over their eyes. Those AI-naïve law-based experts are mistaken about what AI is.

Ouch, we seem to have once again arrived at the notion that AI-in-the-law is inextricably two things mixed together and you've got to be on your top game for both.

Section 3: Conclusion

You might be tempted to draw a straw and say that AI-in-the-law should be in law schools. The problem this presents is that it can be viewed as an oddball or outcast in some law schools. The AI elements are not especially given much legal-minded credit. Law schools often revere specialties within the field of law, such as being a specialist in constitutional law, family law, tax law, maritime law, or whatever.

The law school faculty member or researcher that focuses entirely on AI-in-the-law is seen as a jack of all trades but a master of none. Hopes of advancing within the law school are often dim. This might gradually, slowly, and at a snail's pace change, especially as AI-in-the-law gets bigger and bigger overall in the eyes of society. For now, it is a tough sell.

Some have valiantly tried to make a safe spot for AI-in-the-law as becoming a permanent and welcomed resident in law schools.

For example, an intriguing research paper by Thomas Gordon proposed that AI-in-the-law is rightfully a strident member of legal theory and ergo law schools ought to solidify around this: "AI and Law should become part of legal theory, or rather a "school" of legal theory, to enable the field to eventually become an integral part of legal education and academic legal research" (in his thought-provoking paper of 2005 entitled "Artificial Intelligence and Legal Theory at Law Schools"). Regrettably, this suggestion has not especially materialized, though admirable props go to the idea of it.

All right, if the law schools aren't clamoring for AI-in-the-law, we'll walk across the street and hand the matter to computer science departments. Surely, they will grab up the hot topic.

I don't want to be the bearer of demoralizing news, but AI-in-the-law within computer science departments is not necessarily a grabber either. Computer science typically seeks to expand the field of computer science, naturally so, by exploring new theories of computing and algorithmic capacities. Unless the domain of law is going to clearly bring forth those delights, the AI-in-the-law is a pat on the back nicety but nothing more so.

It seems that AI-in-the-law is caught in that in-between zone. Not exactly the best fit for law schools, and not exactly the best fit for computer science.

Another problematic issue that some decry is that even if AI-in-the-law was somehow officially anointed as residing only in one of those areas and therefore finally having a resolute home, you would likely soon see the field die off or at least stagnate.

The logic is that the particular domain would dominate this intersecting brotherhood. In a law school, the AI would be a second fiddle and the law aspects would override anything else. In a computer science department, the AI would be the keystone and meanwhile, the law aspects would be given short shrift.

All in all, the vexing matter is like that proverbial fish out of water. The thing is, there doesn't seem to be any proper pool of water into which this fish can exist and thrive.

We aren't likely to settle this enduring quandary right now. The approach generally taken is that sometimes AI-in-the-law lands in a law school and does well, or it lands in computer science and does well, or it doesn't find a resident home and has to quietly exist in a borderline manner.

Kudos to those courageous enough to tackle AI-in-the-law, no matter which home you manage to find and no matter what confusion or consternation this might provoke by those that say it ought to be in some other place.

The sage remark comes to mind that home is wherever your heart resides.

Note: *For supplemental materials depicting the aspects discussed in this chapter, refer to Appendix B, which contains various augmented diagrams, charts, and additional related facets of relevance.*

CHAPTER 25
AI & LAW: MECHANIZATION PHRASING

Key briefing points about this essay:

- Earlier on, some thought the catchphrase of "mechanized lawyering" might catch on
- We used to view something being mechanized as futuristic and advanced
- No more, with instead "automation" stepping into the popularity ring
- Topping the automation moniker has become the use of AI
- AI-in-the-law is gaining speed and increasingly being applied to many legal uses

Section 1: Introduction

Mechanization is an interesting word.

It used to be that to say that something had been mechanized was a kind of futuristic phrasing.

You were seemingly going beyond the norm and extending human by-hand efforts into a near sci-fi realm. During World War I, the notion of mechanized warfare first really became widely seen via the use of armored tanks, and of course, by World War II there were plenty of mechanized armaments and military efforts afoot. Historians have a bit of consternation about pointing to WWI and WWII as mechanization highlights since you can trace mechanization much further back in history, assuming that you are more lenient on what mechanization denotes.

We also all know about the rise of mechanization in factories and assembly plants.

A worker would be augmented by some form of mechanical device and thus be able to do many times more work effort in a likely even shorter amount of time. This tended to mean that a factory could hire fewer workers, or perhaps lay off workers, causing a lot of hand wringing about what mechanization would do to livelihoods.

I dare say that today the idea of mechanizing a work aspect is perceived as a bit old-fashioned. You don't mechanize endeavors anymore. You automate endeavors.

The connotation of automation seems to include that you might entirely replace the use of human labor from a given process. Mechanization does not usually have that same all-told implication. Sure, you can stretch the mechanization moniker to encompass turning action into being fully automated and taking humans completely out of the loop, though few today would describe this as being "mechanized" per se.

Why do I bring up this bit of semantic analysis about the mechanizing overtones and undertones?

Because of the application of computer-based systems to legal tasks and the practice of law, for which there was at one time a keen interest in describing as a form of mechanization.

Here's what some *used* to be saying was taking place via the advent of advanced computing:

- Mechanization of the law
- Mechanized lawyers
- Mechanized lawyering
- Etc.

Section 2: Mechanized As A Lexicon

I believe that one of the earliest outright proposals to adopt such phrasing might have appeared in a 2014 paper entitled "Computational Law: Law That Works Like Software" that was authored by Hans Andersson. In short, he mentions this salient aspect: "Mechanized Lawyering will describe the machine-oriented automation of a set of workflows specific to lawyering, for instance, due diligence in the context of a corporate acquisition. Mechanized lawyering might (but not necessarily) employ legal informatics, but whereas legal informatics focuses on the role of information, mechanized lawyering focuses on the processes by which lawyers practice."

A quick scan of the subsequent literature suggests that the catchphrase of "mechanized" when attached to the law, lawyers, lawyering, and the like has rarely occurred. In addition, if you take even a cursory look at the LegalTech marketplace today, seldom would you observe any pronouncements about a vendor tool having aided in *mechanizing* the practice of law.

What happened to the law-oriented mechanization lexicon?

One interpretation is that mechanization gave way to a more preferred facet of referring to *automation.*

You see, automation is cooler. Also, automation seems to include both partially automating a legal task and also potentially fully automating it. Furthermore, as AI has gotten stronger as an *automating capacity,* there is a great deal of anticipation that AI will ultimately be able to autonomously perform legal tasks and carry out bona fide legal reasoning akin to human lawyers.

Even automation as a catchword is starting to become a bit unfashionable. Rather than focusing on automation as a keyword, many refer instead to AI-in-the-law or use a similar flavor of phrasing about the advent of AI being infused into the law.

I'd like to make sure to straighten out what it means to refer to AI-in-the-law. I say this because many are often taking a lopsided or narrow view of what the realm consists of.

Please know that there are two major ways to intertwine AI and the law: (1) AI as applied to the law and the practice of law, (2) Law as applied to the advent of AI.

In the first instance, lawyers and legal scholars emphasize the use of AI as applied to the law, which I'll signify as the so-called robo-lawyer, robo-judge, robo-juror, and the like kinds of aspirations. Note that I am not a fan of that robo verbiage, but it is admittedly a quick way to invoke the imagery of what applied AI is ultimately aiming to do.

The second instance consists of applying the law to AI, such as ascertaining how our laws and regulations should be adjusted or crafted anew to cope with the burgeoning use of AI throughout society. This is construed as using legal acumen to figure out the appropriate means of governing AI.

Let's noodle on this for a brief moment.

Much of the flashy aspects about AI-in-the-law stems from the application of AI into the law (that's the first case indicated above). Especially popular ways of applying AI in the law consist of infusing Natural Language Processing (NLP) capabilities into the arduous chore of doing e-Discovery (i.e., AI-based NLP is especially useful when dealing with large-scale narrative-oriented datasets that require extensive and otherwise laborious by-hand legal discovery efforts). And you are perhaps familiar with the use of AI for aiding in examining and composing legal contracts. There are lots of these infusions taking place of plopping AI techniques and technologies into the carrying out bona fide legal tasks.

I'd almost bet that you were probably thinking of AI-in-the-law as purely the application of AI to the law.

Time to expand that way of thinking.

Get ready for the next boon, namely the need to apply the law to AI. This is gradually gaining notable ground and outstretched headlines. Why so? This is partially due to the rampant and uncontrolled promulgating of AI that has showcased seedy and untoward capacities. The recent era of AI began with a rousing cheer that AI would be abundantly good for society, but quickly discovered that there is the grimy underbelly of AI too. AI systems are now suspect right away, often embedding contemptible biases in factors such as race, gender, etc. As a result, the applying of the law to AI is garnering a lot of steam.

Section 3: Conclusion

Returning to the mechanization versus automation nomenclature debate, we can pretty much put to bed the mechanized wording. This seems nearly extinct and unlikely to regain any notable traction.

Automation is still a commonly used catchphrase. It though borderlines on being outdated, akin to trendy clothing lines that eventually lose their cultural pizzazz. AI is in. The odds are that AI is going to get the lion's share of the word salad that comes up when discussing the automating of lawyering or lawyer-like tasks.

These seem to be gaining in popularity:

- AI-infused lawyering
- AI-based lawyer
- AI-powered legal capabilities
- Etc.

We've not turned the corner toward robo-lawyer or robo-lawyering as being well-accepted. The robo labeling is typically touted in eyeball-seeking headlines and by vendors that at times overstep and wish to garner outsized attention.

Meanwhile, mechanized seems to have been put out to pasture. Sorry, mechanized, but you did get your fifteen minutes of fame earlier on and can fondly recall those days of being in the.

.

Note: *For supplemental materials depicting the aspects discussed in this chapter, refer to Appendix B, which contains various augmented diagrams, charts, and additional related facets of relevance*

APPENDIX A

TEACHING WITH THIS MATERIAL AND BIBLIOGRAPHY

The essays in this book can readily be used as a reading supplemental to augment traditional textbook-oriented content, particularly used in a class on AI or a class about the law.

Courses where this material is most likely applicable encompass classes at a college or university level.

Here are some typical settings that might apply:

- Computer Science. Classes studying AI, or possibly a CS social impacts class, etc.

- Law. Law classes exploring technology and its adoption for legal uses.

- Sociology. Sociology classes on the adoption and advancement of technology.

Specialized classes at the undergraduate and graduate level can also make use of this material.

For each chapter, consider whether you think the chapter provides material relevant to your course topic.

There are plenty of opportunities to get the students thinking about the topics and encourage them to decide whether they agree or disagree with the points offered and positions taken.

I would also encourage you to have the students do additional research beyond the chapter material presented (I provide next some suggested assignments that they can do).

RESEARCH ASSIGNMENTS ON THESE TOPICS

Your students can find research and background material on these topics, doing so in various tech journals, law journals, and other related publications.

Here are some suggestions for homework or projects that you could assign to students:

a) Assignment for foundational AI research topics: Research and prepare a paper and a presentation on a specific aspect of AI, such as Machine Learning, ANN, etc. The paper should cite at least 3 reputable sources. Compare and contrast to what has been stated in the chosen chapter.

b) Assignment for Law topics: Research and prepare a paper covering Law aspects via at least 3 reputable sources and analyze the characterizations. Compare and contrast to what has been stated in the chosen chapter.

c) Assignment for a Business topic: Research and prepare a paper and a presentation on businesses and advanced technology regarding AI and Law. What is trending, and why? Make sure to cite at least 3 reputable sources. Compare and contrast to the depictions herein.

d) Assignment to do a Startup: Have the students prepare a paper or business plan about how they might start up a business in this realm. They could also be asked to present their business plan and should also have a prepared presentation deck to coincide with it.

You can certainly adjust the aforementioned assignments to fit your particular needs and class structure.

You'll notice that I usually suggest that (at least) 3 reputable cited sources be utilized for the paper writing-based assignments.

I usually steer students toward "reputable" publications, since otherwise, they will cite some less reliable sources that have little or no credentials, other than that they happened to appear online was easy to retrieve. You can, of course, define "reputable" in whatever way you prefer, for example, some faculty think Wikipedia is not reputable while others believe it is reputable and allow students to cite it.

The reason that I usually ask for at least 3 citations is that if the student only relies upon one or two citations, they usually settle on whatever they happened to find the fastest. By requiring 3 (or more) citations, it usually seems to inspire them to explore more extensively and likely end-up finding five or more sources, and then whittling it down to 3 if so needed.

I have not specified the length of their papers and leave that to you to tell the students what you prefer.

For each of those assignments, you could end up with a short one to two-pager or you could do a dissertation length in-depth paper. Base the length on whatever best fits for your class, and likewise the credit amount of the assignment within the context of the other grading metrics you'll be using for the class.

I usually try to get students to present their work, in addition to doing the writing. This is a helpful practice for what they will do in the business world. Most of the time, they will be required to prepare an analysis and present it. If you don't have the class time or inclination to have the students present their papers, then you can presumably omit the aspect of them putting together presentations.

GUIDE TO USING THE CHAPTERS

For each of the chapters, I provide the next some various ways to use the chapter contents.

You can assign the below tasks as individual homework assignments, or the tasks can be used for team projects. You can easily layout a series of assignments, such as indicating that the students are to do item "a" below for say Chapter 1, then "b" for the next chapter of the book, and so on.

a) What is the main point of the chapter and describe in your own words the significance of the topic.

b) Identify at least two aspects in the chapter that you agree with and support your concurrence by providing at least one other outside researched item as support; make sure to explain your basis for agreeing with the aspects.

c) Identify at least two aspects in the chapter that you disagree with and support your disagreement by providing at least one other outside researched item as support; make sure to explain your basis for disagreeing with the aspects.

d) Find an aspect that was not covered extensively in the chapter, doing so by conducting outside research, and then offer an expanded indication about how that aspect ties into the chapter, along with the added significance it brings to the topic.

e) Interview a specialist in the industry about the topic of the chapter, collect from them their thoughts and opinions, and readdress the chapter by citing your source and how they compared and contrasted to the material,

f) Interview a relevant professor or researcher in a college or university setting about the topic of the chapter, collect from them their thoughts and opinions, and readdress the chapter by citing your source and how they compared and contrasted to the material,

g) Try to update a chapter by finding out the latest on the topic and ascertain whether the issue or topic has now been solved or whether it is still being addressed, explain what you come up with.

The above are all ways in which you can get the students of your class involved in considering the material of a given chapter. You could mix things up by having one of those above assignments per each week, covering the chapters over the course of the semester or quarter.

SUGGESTED REFERENCES TO EXPLORE

To help get your students started in finding relevant and important papers on the topic of AI and the law, I provide next a handy bibliography that can be utilized.

You could also assign the students to each (or in teams) read an assigned reference from the list, and then have them provide either a written summary and review or do so as part of a classroom presentation.

BIBLIOGRAPHIC REFERENCES

1. Aleven, Vincent (1997). "Teaching Case-Based Argumentation Through a Model and Examples," Ph.D. Dissertation, University of Pittsburgh.

2. Aleven, Vincent (2003). "Using Background Knowledge in Case-Based Legal Reasoning: A Computational Model and an Intelligent Learning Environment," Artificial Intelligence.

3. Amgoud, Leila (2012). "Five Weaknesses of ASPIC+," Volume 299, Communications in Computer and Information Science (CCIS).

4. Antonious, Grigoris, and George Baryannis, Sotiris Batsakis, Guido Governatori, Livio Robaldo, Givoanni Siragusa, Ilias Tachmazidis (2018). "Legal Reasoning and Big Data: Opportunities and Challenges," August 2018, MIREL Workshop on Mining and Reasoning Legal Texts.

5. Ashley, Kevin (1991). "Reasoning with Cases and Hypotheticals in HYPO," Volume 34, International Journal of Man-Machine Studies.

6. Ashley, Kevin, and Karl Branting, Howard Margolis, and Cass Sunstein (2001). "Legal Reasoning and Artificial Intelligence: How Computers 'Think' Like Lawyers," Symposium: Legal Reasoning and Artificial Intelligence, University of Chicago Law School Roundtable.

7. Baker, Jamie (2018). "A Legal Research Odyssey: Artificial Intelligence as Disrupter," Law Library Journal.

8. Batsakis, Sotiris, and George Baryannis, Guido Governatori, Illias Tachmazidis, Grigoris Antoniou (2018). "Legal Representation and Reasoning in Practice: A Critical Comparison," Volume 313, Legal Knowledge and Information Systems.

9. Bench-Capon, Trevor (2004). "AGATHA: Automation of the Construction of Theories in Case Law Domains," January 2004, Legal Knowledge and Information Systems Jurix 2004, Amsterdam.

10. Bench-Capon, Trevor (2012). "Representing Popov v Hayashi with Dimensions and Factors," March 2012, Artificial Intelligence and Law.

11. Bench-Capon, Trevor, and Givoanni Sartor (2003). "A Model of Legal Reasoning with Cases Incorporating Theories and Values," November 2013, Artificial Intelligence.

12. Breuker, Joost (1996). "A Functional Ontology of Law," October 1996, ResearchGate.

13. Bruninghaus, Stefanie, and Kevin Ashley (2003). "Combining Case-Based and Model-Based Reasoning for Predicting the Outcome of Legal Cases," June 2003, ICCBR'03: Proceedings of the 5th International Conference on Case-based reasoning: Research and Development.

14. Buchanan, Bruce, and Thomas Headrick (1970). "Some Speculation about Artificial Intelligence and Legal Reasoning," Volume 23, Stanford Law Review.

15. Chagal-Feferkorn, Karni (2019). "Am I An Algorithm or a Product: When Products Liability Should Apply to Algorithmic Decision-Makers," Stanford Law & Policy Review.

16. Douglas, William (1948). "The Dissent: A Safeguard of Democracy," Volume 32, Journal of the American Judicature Society.

17. Dung, P, and R. Kowalski, F. Toni (2006). "Dialectic Proof Procedures for Assumption-Based Admissible Argumentation," Artificial Intelligence.

18. Eliot, Lance (2020). AI And Legal Reasoning Essentials. LBE Press Publishing.

19. Eliot, Lance (2020). Artificial Intelligence and LegalTech Essentials. LBE Press Publishing.

20. Eliot, Lance (2020). "FutureLaw 2020 Showcases How Tech is Transforming The Law, Including the Impacts of AI," April 16, 2020, Forbes.

21. Erdem, Esra, and Michael Gelfond, Nicola Leone (2016). "Applications of Answer Set Programming," AI Magazine.

22. Gardner, Anne (1987). Artificial Intelligence and Legal Reasoning. MIT Press.

23. Genesereth, Michael (2009). "Computational Law: The Cop in the Backseat," Stanford Center for Legal Informatics, Stanford University.

24. Ghosh, Mirna (2019). "Automation of Legal Reasoning and Decision Based on Ontologies," Normandie Universite.

25. Grabmair, Matthias (2017). "Predicting Trade Secret Case Outcomes using Argument Schemes and Learned Quantitative Value Effect Tradeoffs," IJCAI June 12, 2017, London, United Kingdom.

26. Hage, Jaap (1996). "A Theory of Legal Reasoning and a Logic to Match," Volume 4, Artificial Intelligence and Law.

27. Hage, Jaap (2000). "Dialectical Models in Artificial Intelligence and Law," Artificial Intelligence and Law.

28. Hage, Japp, and Ronald Leenes, Arno Lodder (1993). "Hard Cases: A Procedural Approach," Artificial Intelligence and Law.

29. Hobbes, Thomas (1651). The Matter, Form, and Power of a Common-Wealth Ecclesiasticall and Civil.

30. Holmes, Oliver (1897). "The Path of the Law," Volume 10, Harvard Law Review.

31. Katz, Daniel, and Michael Bommarito, Josh Blackman (2017). "A General Approach for Predicting the Behavior of the Supreme Court of the United States," April 12, 2017, PLOS ONE.

32. Kowalski, Robert, and Francesca Toni (1996). "Abstract Argumentation," AI-Law96.

33. Laswell, Harold (1955). "Current Studies of the Decision Process: Automation Creativity," Volume 8, Western Political Quarterly.

34. Libal, Tomer, and Alexander Steen (2019). "The NAI Suite: Drafting and Reasoning over Legal Texts," October 15, 2019, arXiv.

35. Lipton, Zachary (2017). "The Mythos of Model Interpretability," March 6, 2017, arXiv.

36. Martin, Andrew, and Kevin Quinn, Theodore Ruger, Pauline Kim (2004). "Competing Approaches to Predicting Supreme Court Decision Making," December 2014, Symposium on Forecasting U.S. Supreme Court Decisions.

37. McCarty, Thorne (1977). "Reflections on TAXMAN: An Experiment in Artificial Intelligence and Legal Reasoning," January 1977, Harvard Law Review.

38. Modgil, Sanjay, and Henry Prakken (2013). "The ASPIC+ Framework for Structured Argumentation: A Tutorial," December 16, 2013, Argument & Computation.

39. Mowbray, Andrew, and Philip Chung, Graham Greenleaf (2019). "Utilising AI in the Legal Assistance Sector," LegalAIIA Workshop, ICAIL, June 17, 2019, Montreal, Canada.

40. Parasuraman, Raja, and Thomas Sheridan, Christopher Wickens (2000). "A Model for Types and Levels of Human Interaction with Automation," May 2000, IEEE Transactions on Systems, Man, and Cybernetics.

41. Popple, James (1993). "SHYSTER: A Pragmatic Legal Expert System," Ph.D. Dissertation, Australian National University.

42. Prakken, Henry, and Giovanni Sartor (2015). "Law and Logic: A Review from an Argumentation Perspective," Volume 227, Artificial Intelligence.

43. Rissland, Edwina (1988). Artificial Intelligence and Legal Reasoning: A Discussion of the Field and Gardner's Book," Volume 9, AI Magazine.

44. Rissland, Edwina (1990). "Artificial Intelligence and Law: Stepping Stones to a Model of Legal Reasoning," Yale Law Journal.

45. Searle, John (1980). "Minds, Brains, and Programs," Volume 3, Behavioral and Brain Sciences.

46. Sunstein, Cass (2001). "Of Artificial Intelligence and Legal Reasoning," University of Chicago Law School, Public Law and Legal Theory Working Papers.

47. Sunstein, Cass, and Kevin Ashley, Karl Branting, Howard Margolis (2001). "Legal Reasoning and Artificial Intelligence: How Computers 'Think' Like Lawyers," Symposium: Legal Reasoning and Artificial Intelligence, University of Chicago Law School Roundtable.

48. Surden, Harry (2014). "Machine Learning and Law," Washington Law Review.

49. Surden, Harry (2019). "Artificial Intelligence and Law: An Overview," Summer 2019, Georgia State University Law Review.

50. Valente, Andre, and Joost Breuker (1996). "A Functional Ontology of Law," Artificial Intelligence and Law.

51. Waltl, Bernhard, and Roland Vogl (2018). "Explainable Artificial Intelligence: The New Frontier in Legal Informatics," February 2018, Jusletter IT 22, Stanford Center for Legal Informatics, Stanford University.

52. Wittgenstein, Ludwig (1953). Philosophical Investigations. Blackwell Publishing.

APPENDIX B
SUPPLEMENTAL FIGURES AND CHARTS

For the convenience of viewing, supplemental figures and charts related to the topics discussed are shown on the next pages

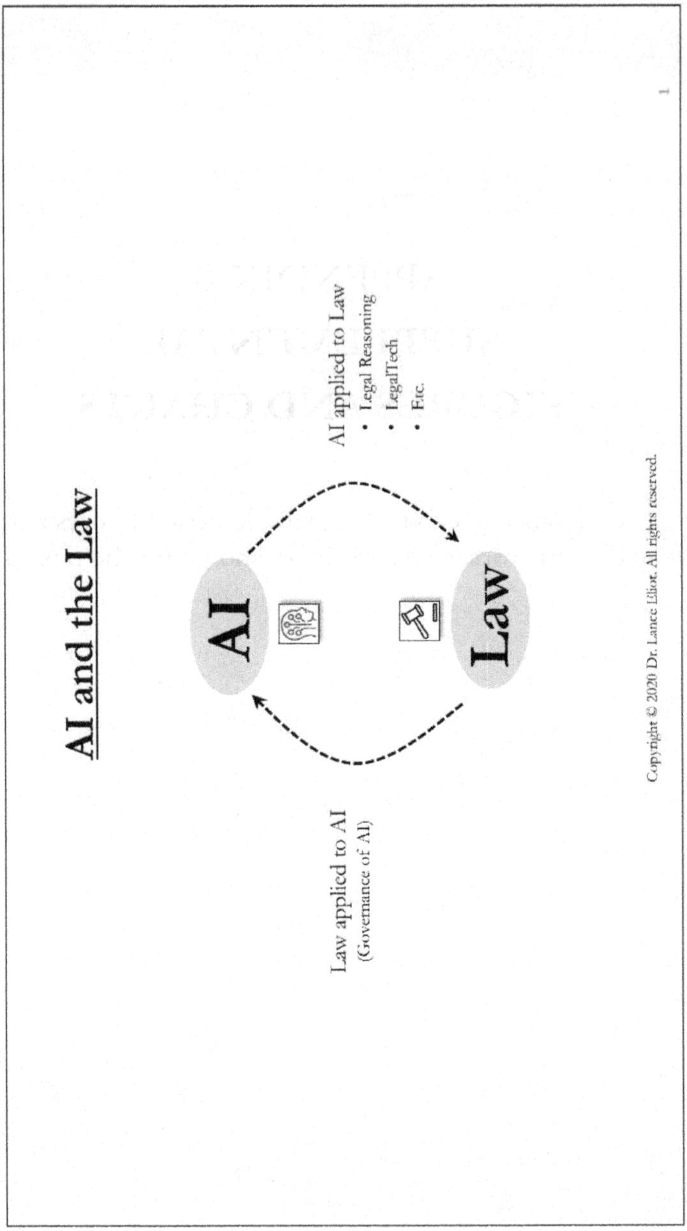
AI and the Law
AI
Law
AI applied to Law
• Legal Reasoning
• LegalTech
• Etc.
Law applied to AI
(Governance of AI)
Copyright © 2020 Dr. Lance Eliot. All rights reserved.
1

Figure 1

AI & Law: Levels of Autonomy For AI Legal Reasoning (AILR)

Level	Descriptor	Examples	Automation	Status
0	No Automation	Manual, paper-based (no automation)	None	De Facto - In Use
1	Simple Assistance Automation	Word Processing, XLS, online legal docs, etc.	Legal Assist	Widely In Use
2	Advanced Assistance Automation	Query-style NLP, ML for case prediction, etc.	Legal Assist	Some In Use
3	Semi-Autonomous Automation	KBS & ML/DL for legal reasoning & analysis, etc.	Legal Assist	Primarily Prototypes & Research Based
4	AILR Domain Autonomous	Versed only in a specific legal domain	Legal Advisor (law fluent)	None As Yet
5	AILR Fully Autonomous	Versatile within and across all legal domains	Legal Advisor (law fluent)	None As Yet
6	AILR Superhuman Autonomous	Exceeds human-based legal reasoning	Supra Legal Advisor	Indeterminate

Figure 1: AI & Law - Autonomous Levels by Rows

Source Author: Dr. Lance B. Eliot

V1.3

Figure 2

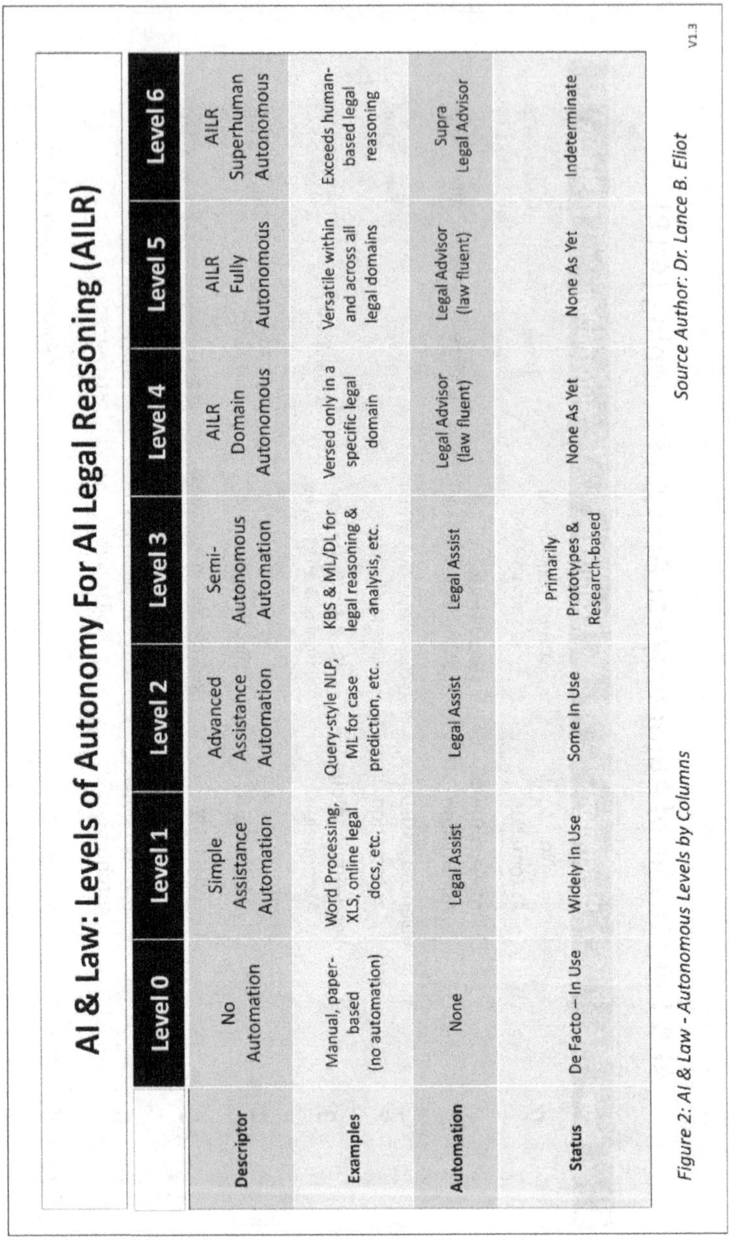

AI & Law: Levels of Autonomy For AI Legal Reasoning (AILR)

	Level 0	Level 1	Level 2	Level 3	Level 4	Level 5	Level 6
Descriptor	No Automation	Simple Assistance Automation	Advanced Assistance Automation	Semi-Autonomous Automation	AILR Domain Autonomous	AILR Fully Autonomous	AILR Superhuman Autonomous
Examples	Manual, paper-based (no automation)	Word Processing, XLS, online legal docs, etc.	Query-style NLP, ML for case prediction, etc.	KBS & ML/DL for legal reasoning & analysis, etc.	Versed only in a specific legal domain	Versatile within and across all legal domains	Exceeds human-based legal reasoning
Automation	None	Legal Assist	Legal Assist	Legal Assist	Legal Advisor (law fluent)	Legal Advisor (law fluent)	Supra Legal Advisor
Status	De Facto – In Use	Widely In Use	Some In Use	Primarily Prototypes & Research-based	None As Yet	None As Yet	Indeterminate

Figure 2: AI & Law - Autonomous Levels by Columns

Source Author: Dr. Lance B. Eliot

V1.3

Figure 3

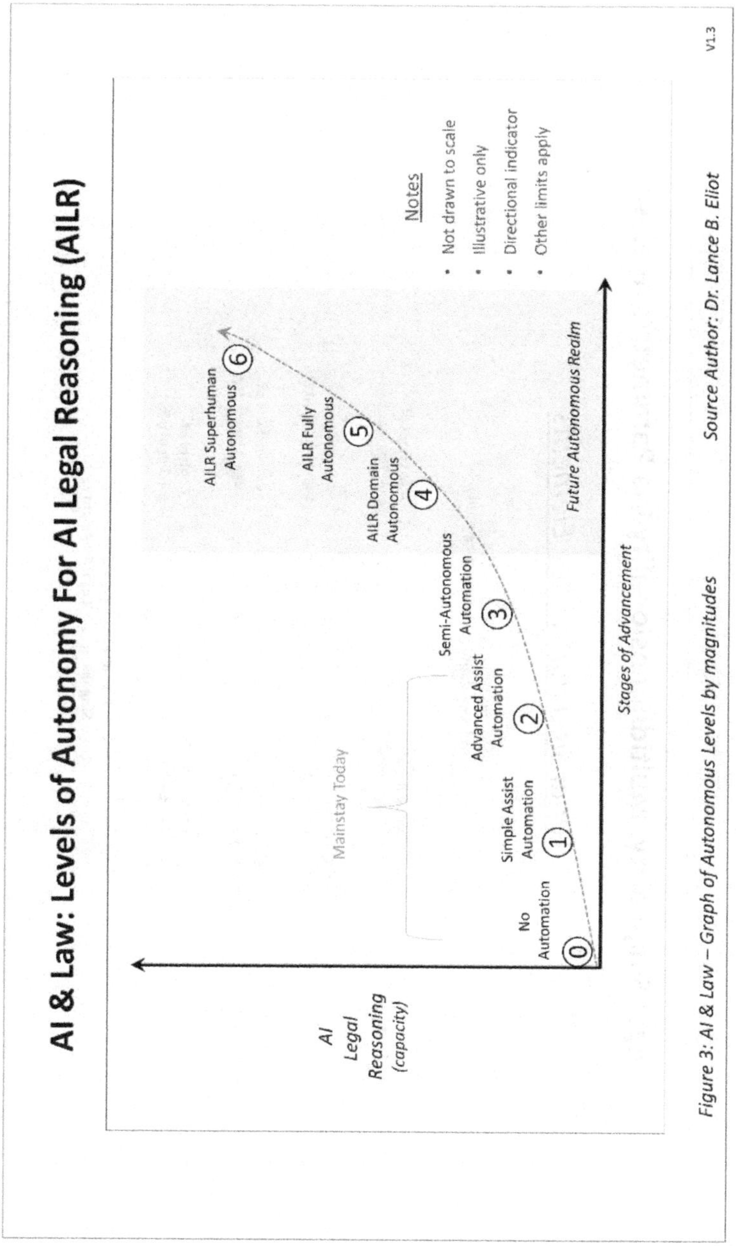

Figure 3: AI & Law – Graph of Autonomous Levels by magnitudes   *Source Author: Dr. Lance B. Eliot*

Figure 4

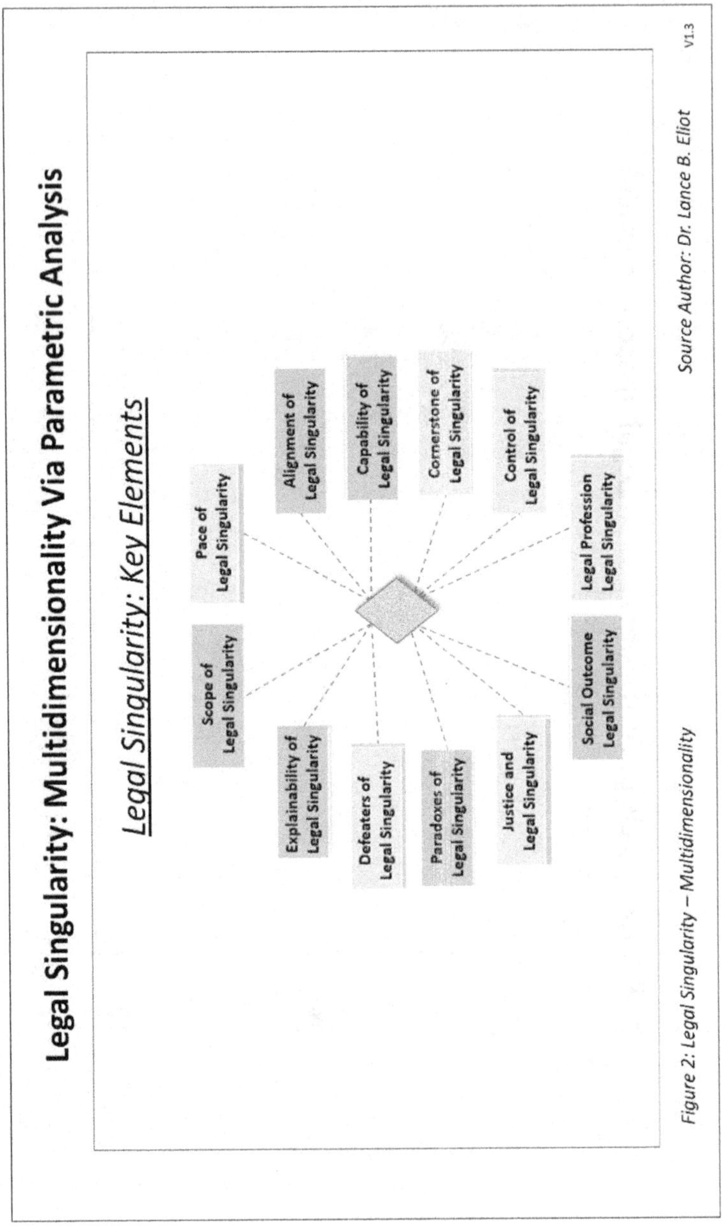
Legal Singularity: Multidimensionality Via Parametric Analysis
Legal Singularity: Key Elements
Scope of Legal Singularity
Pace of Legal Singularity
Alignment of Legal Singularity
Capability of Legal Singularity
Cornerstone of Legal Singularity
Control of Legal Singularity
Legal Profession Legal Singularity
Social Outcome Legal Singularity
Justice and Legal Singularity
Paradoxes of Legal Singularity
Defeaters of Legal Singularity
Explainability of Legal Singularity
Figure 2: Legal Singularity – Multidimensionality
Source Author: Dr. Lance B. Eliot
V1.3

Figure 5

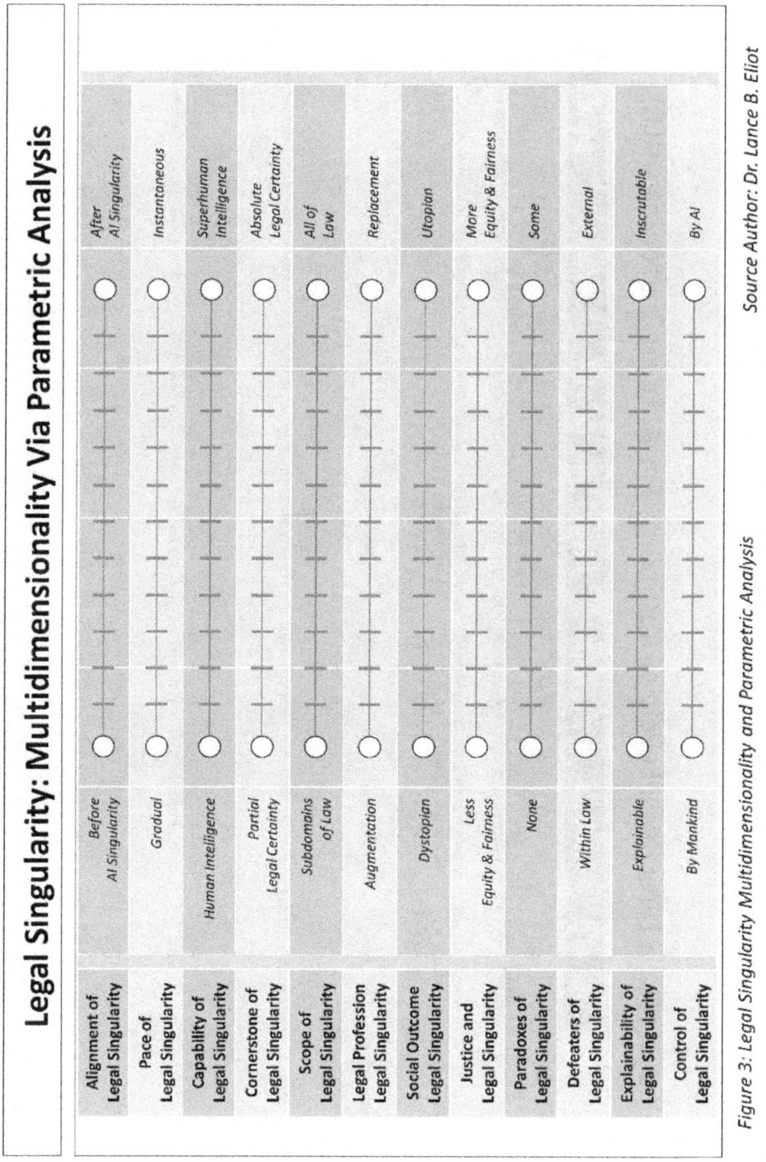
Legal Singularity: Multidimensionality Via Parametric Analysis
Alignment of Legal Singularity
Before AI Singularity
After AI Singularity
Pace of Legal Singularity
Gradual
Instantaneous
Capability of Legal Singularity
Human Intelligence
Superhuman Intelligence
Cornerstone of Legal Singularity
Partial Legal Certainty
Absolute Legal Certainty
Scope of Legal Singularity
Subdomains of Law
All of Law
Legal Profession Legal Singularity
Augmentation
Replacement
Social Outcome Legal Singularity
Dystopian
Utopian
Justice and Legal Singularity
Less Equity & Fairness
More Equity & Fairness
Paradoxes of Legal Singularity
None
Some
Defeaters of Legal Singularity
Within Law
External
Explainability of Legal Singularity
Explainable
Inscrutable
Control of Legal Singularity
By Mankind
By AI
Figure 3: Legal Singularity Multidimensionality and Parametric Analysis
Source Author: Dr. Lance B. Eliot

Figure 6

Legal Micro-Directives: Levels of Autonomy For AI Legal Reasoning (AILR)

	Level 0	Level 1	Level 2	Level 3	Level 4	Level 5	Level 6
Descriptor	No Automation	Simple Assistance Automation	Advanced Assistance Automation	Semi-Autonomous Automation	AILR Domain Autonomous	AILR Fully Autonomous	AILR Superhuman Autonomous
Examples	Manual, paper-based (no automation)	Word Processing, XLS, online legal docs, etc.	Query-style NLP, ML for case prediction, etc.	KBS & ML/DL for legal reasoning & analysis, etc.	Versed only in a specific legal domain	Versatile within and across all legal domains	Exceeds human-based legal reasoning
Automation	None	Legal Assist	Legal Assist	Legal Assist	Legal Advisor (law fluent)	Legal Advisor (law fluent)	Supra Legal Advisor
Status	De Facto – In Use	Widely In Use	Some In Use	Primarily Prototypes & Research-based	None As Yet	None As Yet	Indeterminate
AI-Enabled Legal Micro-Directives	*n/a*	*Impractical*	*Incubatory*	*Infancy*	*Narrow*	*Wide*	*Consummate*

Figure 1: Legal Micro-Directives - Autonomous Levels of AILR by Columns   *Source Author: Dr. Lance B. Eliot*   V1.3

Figure 7

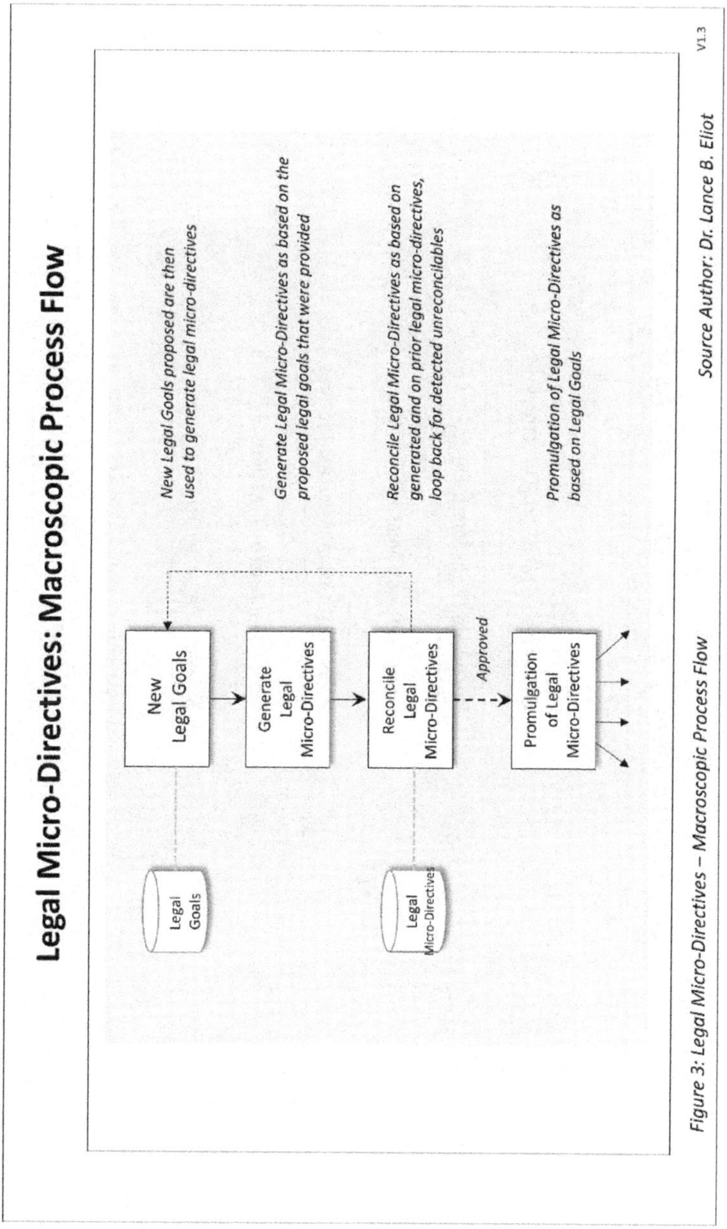
Legal Micro-Directives: Macroscopic Process Flow
Legal Goals
Legal Micro-Directives
New Legal Goals
Generate Legal Micro-Directives
Reconcile Legal Micro-Directives
Approved
Promulgation of Legal Micro-Directives
New Legal Goals proposed are then used to generate legal micro-directives
Generate Legal Micro-Directives as based on the proposed legal goals that were provided
Reconcile Legal Micro-Directives as based on generated and on prior legal micro-directives, loop back for detected unreconcilables
Promulgation of Legal Micro-Directives as based on Legal Goals
Figure 3: Legal Micro-Directives – Macroscopic Process Flow
Source Author: Dr. Lance B. Eliot
V1.3

Figure 8

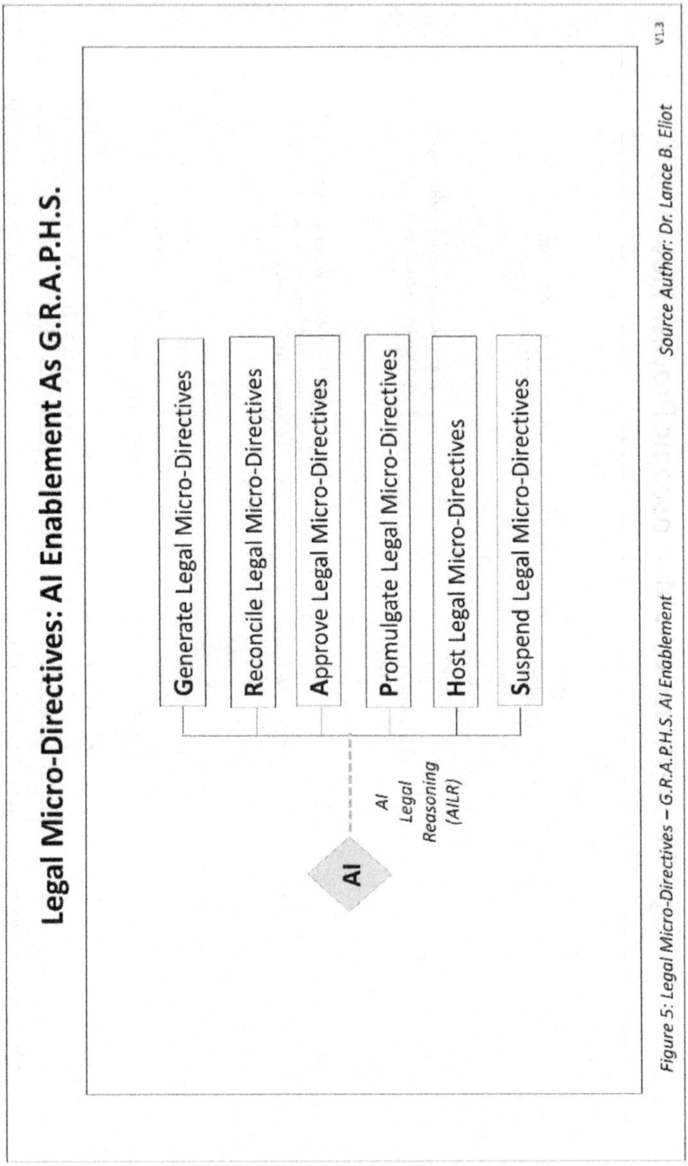
Legal Micro-Directives: AI Enablement As G.R.A.P.H.S.
AI
AI Legal Reasoning (AILR)
Generate Legal Micro-Directives
Reconcile Legal Micro-Directives
Approve Legal Micro-Directives
Promulgate Legal Micro-Directives
Host Legal Micro-Directives
Suspend Legal Micro-Directives
Figure 5: Legal Micro-Directives – G.R.A.P.H.S. AI Enablement
Source Author: Dr. Lance B. Eliot
V1.3

Figure 9

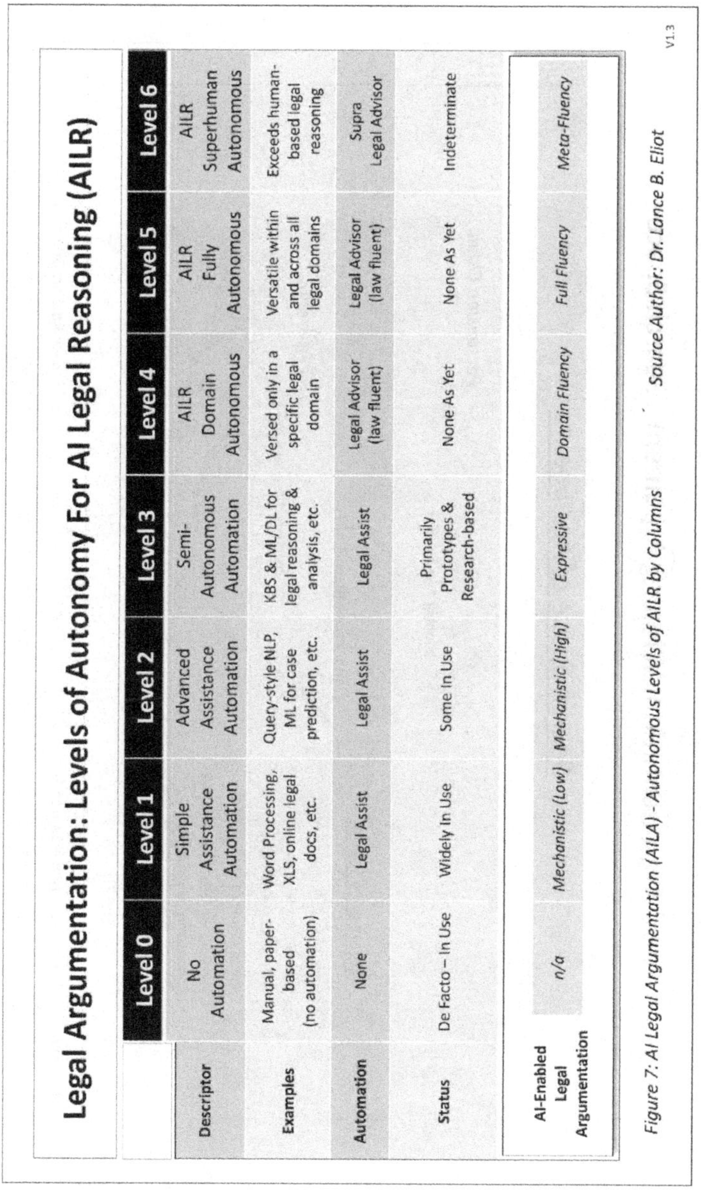

Legal Argumentation: Levels of Autonomy For AI Legal Reasoning (AILR)

	Level 0	Level 1	Level 2	Level 3	Level 4	Level 5	Level 6
Descriptor	No Automation	Simple Assistance Automation	Advanced Assistance Automation	Semi-Autonomous Automation	AILR Domain Autonomous	AILR Fully Autonomous	AILR Superhuman Autonomous
Examples	Manual, paper-based (no automation)	Word Processing, XLS, online legal docs, etc.	Query-style NLP, ML for case prediction, etc.	KBS & ML/DL for legal reasoning & analysis, etc.	Versed only in a specific legal domain	Versatile within and across all legal domains	Exceeds human-based legal reasoning
Automation	None	Legal Assist	Legal Assist	Legal Assist	Legal Advisor (law fluent)	Legal Advisor (law fluent)	Supra Legal Advisor
Status	De Facto – In Use	Widely In Use	Some In Use	Primarily Prototypes & Research-based	None As Yet	None As Yet	Indeterminate
AI-Enabled Legal Argumentation	*n/a*	*Mechanistic (Low)*	*Mechanistic (High)*	*Expressive*	*Domain Fluency*	*Full Fluency*	*Meta-Fluency*

Figure 7: AI Legal Argumentation (AILA) - Autonomous Levels of AILR by Columns *Source Author: Dr. Lance B. Eliot*

V1.3

Figure 10

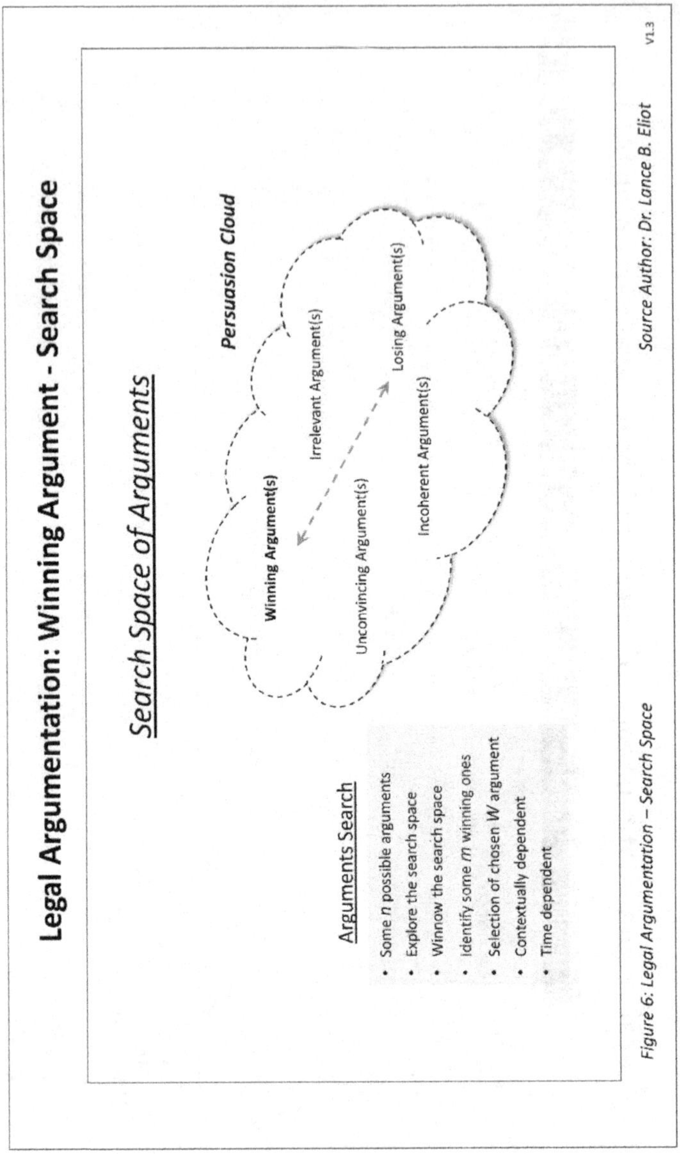
Legal Argumentation: Winning Argument - Search Space
Search Space of Arguments
Persuasion Cloud
Winning Argument(s)
Irrelevant Argument(s)
Losing Argument(s)
Unconvincing Argument(s)
Incoherent Argument(s)
Arguments Search
Some n possible arguments
Explore the search space
Winnow the search space
Identify some m winning ones
Selection of chosen W argument
Contextually dependent
Time dependent
Figure 6: Legal Argumentation – Search Space
Source Author: Dr. Lance B. Eliot
V1.3

Figure 11

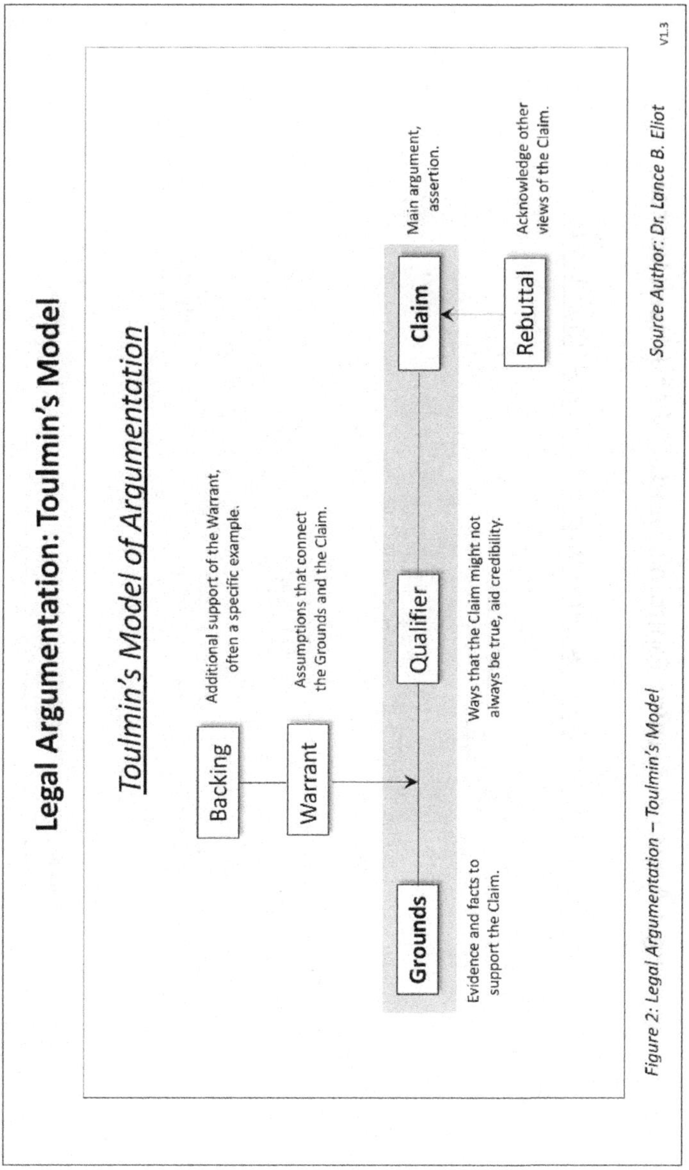
Legal Argumentation: Toulmin's Model
Toulmin's Model of Argumentation
Backing
Additional support of the Warrant, often a specific example.
Warrant
Assumptions that connect the Grounds and the Claim.
Grounds
Evidence and facts to support the Claim.
Qualifier
Ways that the Claim might not always be true, aid credibility.
Claim
Main argument, assertion.
Rebuttal
Acknowledge other views of the Claim.
Figure 2: Legal Argumentation – Toulmin's Model
Source Author: Dr. Lance B. Eliot
V1.3

Figure 12

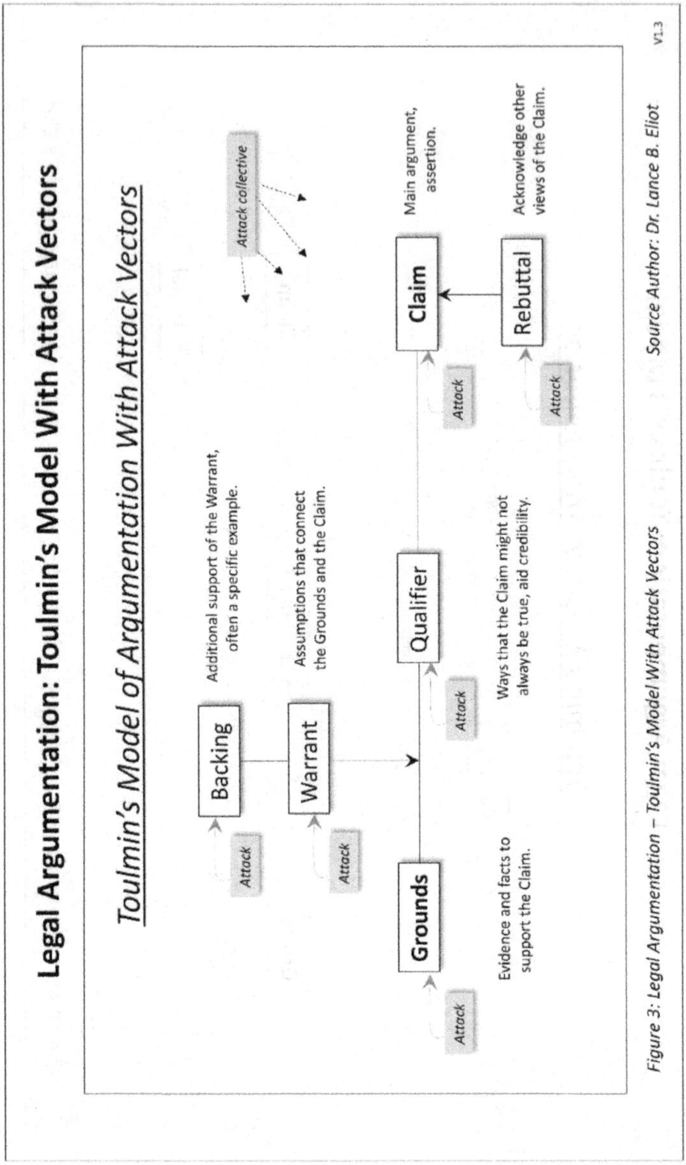
Legal Argumentation: Toulmin's Model With Attack Vectors
Toulmin's Model of Argumentation With Attack Vectors
Attack collective
Backing
Additional support of the Warrant, often a specific example.
Warrant
Assumptions that connect the Grounds and the Claim.
Grounds
Evidence and facts to support the Claim.
Qualifier
Ways that the Claim might not always be true, aid credibility.
Claim
Main argument, assertion.
Rebuttal
Acknowledge other views of the Claim.
Attack
Attack
Attack
Attack
Attack
Attack
Figure 3: Legal Argumentation – Toulmin's Model With Attack Vectors
Source Author: Dr. Lance B. Eliot
V1.3

Figure 13

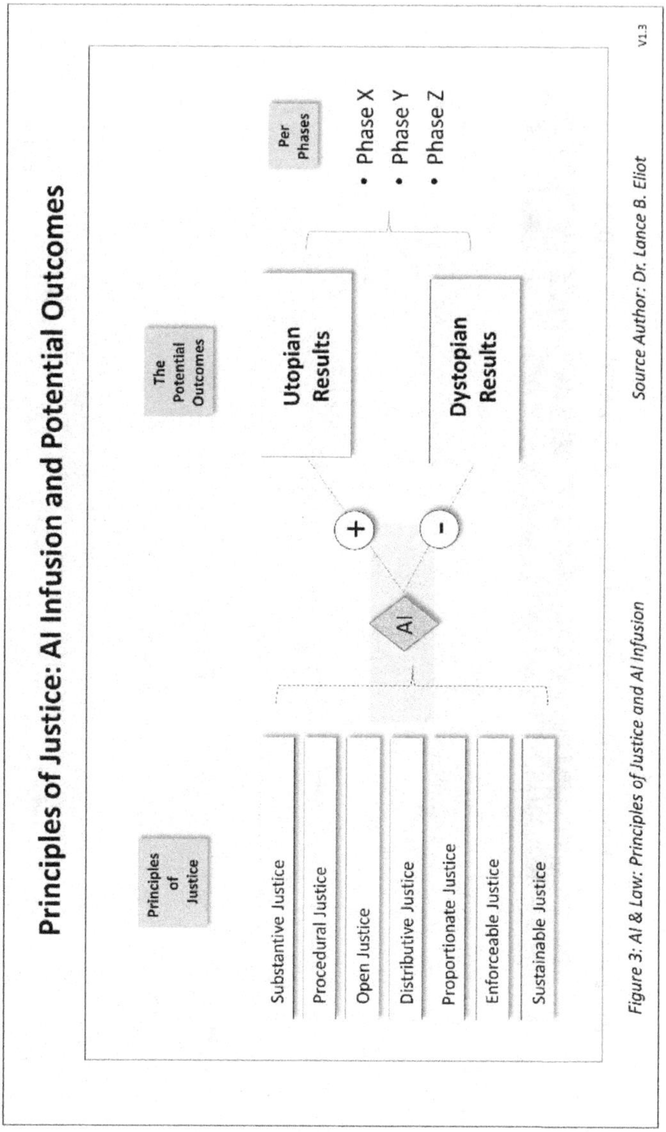
Principles of Justice: AI Infusion and Potential Outcomes
Principles of Justice
The Potential Outcomes
Per Phases
Substantive Justice
Procedural Justice
Open Justice
Distributive Justice
Proportionate Justice
Enforceable Justice
Sustainable Justice
AI
+
-
Utopian Results
Dystopian Results
• Phase X
• Phase Y
• Phase Z
Figure 3: AI & Law: Principles of Justice and AI Infusion
Source Author: Dr. Lance B. Eliot
V1.3

Figure 14

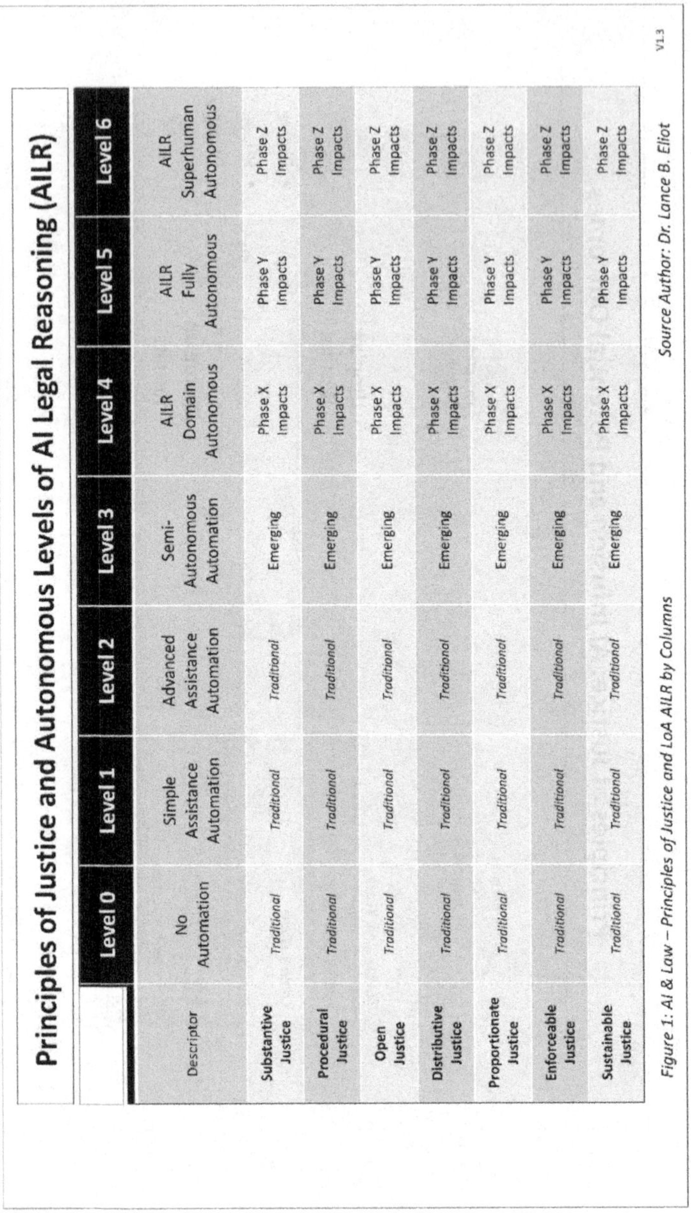

Principles of Justice and Autonomous Levels of AI Legal Reasoning (AILR)

	Level 0	Level 1	Level 2	Level 3	Level 4	Level 5	Level 6
Descriptor	No Automation	Simple Assistance Automation	Advanced Assistance Automation	Semi-Autonomous Automation	AILR Domain Autonomous	AILR Fully Autonomous	AILR Superhuman Autonomous
Substantive Justice	*Traditional*	*Traditional*	*Traditional*	Emerging	Phase X Impacts	Phase Y Impacts	Phase Z Impacts
Procedural Justice	*Traditional*	*Traditional*	*Traditional*	Emerging	Phase X Impacts	Phase Y Impacts	Phase Z Impacts
Open Justice	*Traditional*	*Traditional*	*Traditional*	Emerging	Phase X Impacts	Phase Y Impacts	Phase Z Impacts
Distributive Justice	*Traditional*	*Traditional*	*Traditional*	Emerging	Phase X Impacts	Phase Y Impacts	Phase Z Impacts
Proportionate Justice	*Traditional*	*Traditional*	*Traditional*	Emerging	Phase X Impacts	Phase Y Impacts	Phase Z Impacts
Enforceable Justice	*Traditional*	*Traditional*	*Traditional*	Emerging	Phase X Impacts	Phase Y Impacts	Phase Z Impacts
Sustainable Justice	*Traditional*	*Traditional*	*Traditional*	Emerging	Phase X Impacts	Phase Y Impacts	Phase Z Impacts

Figure 1: AI & Law – Principles of Justice and LoA AILR by Columns

Source Author: Dr. Lance B. Eliot

V1.3

Figure 15

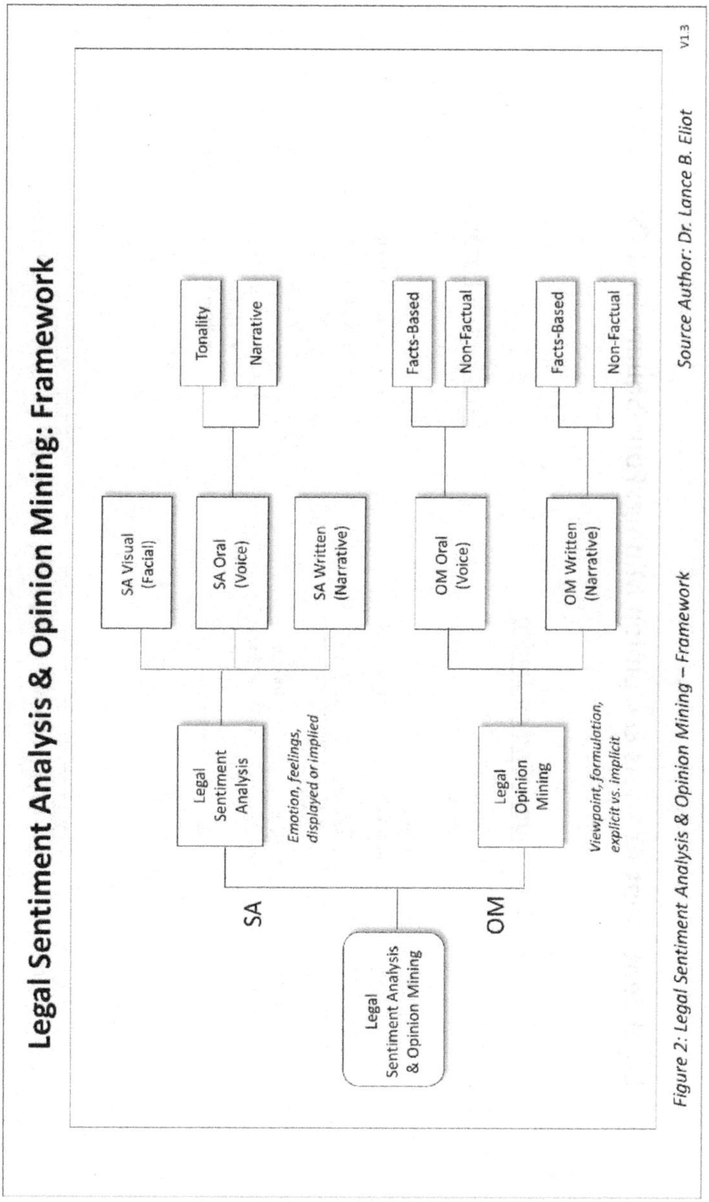
Legal Sentiment Analysis & Opinion Mining: Framework
Legal Sentiment Analysis & Opinion Mining
SA
OM
Legal Sentiment Analysis
Emotion, feelings, displayed or implied
Legal Opinion Mining
Viewpoint, formulation, explicit vs. implicit
SA Visual (Facial)
SA Oral (Voice)
SA Written (Narrative)
OM Oral (Voice)
OM Written (Narrative)
Tonality
Narrative
Facts-Based
Non-Factual
Facts-Based
Non-Factual
Figure 2: Legal Sentiment Analysis & Opinion Mining – Framework
Source Author: Dr. Lance B. Eliot
V1.3

Figure 16

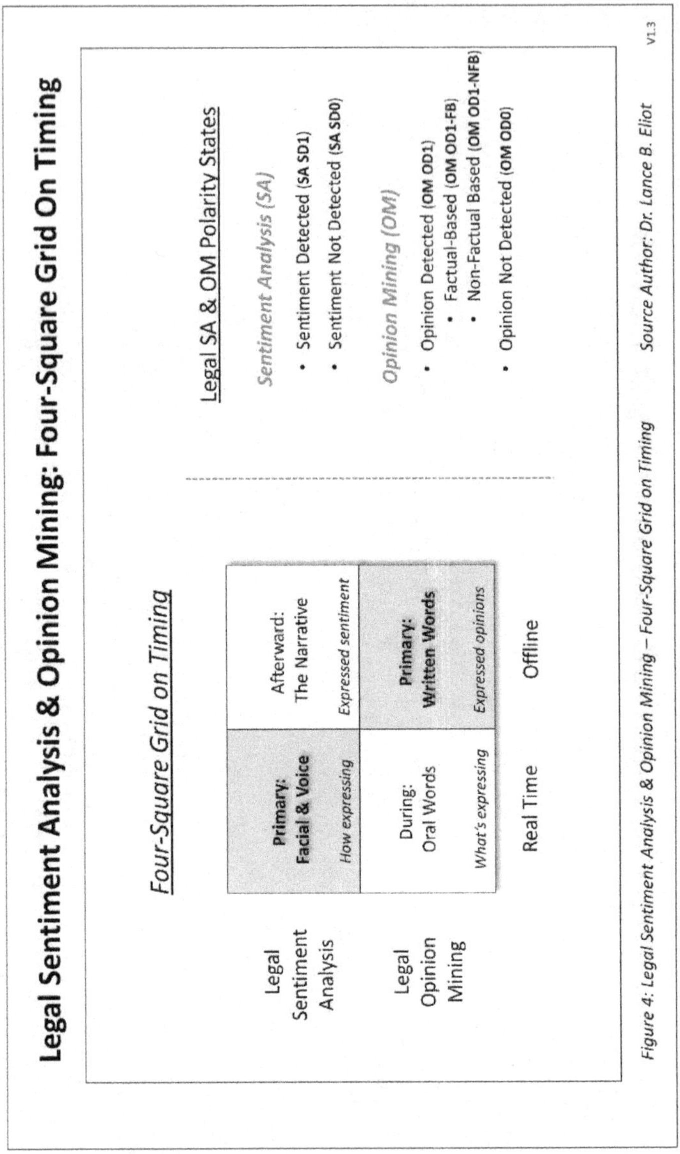
Legal Sentiment Analysis & Opinion Mining: Four-Square Grid On Timing
Four-Square Grid on Timing
Legal Sentiment Analysis
Legal Opinion Mining
Primary: Facial & Voice
How expressing
Afterward: The Narrative
Expressed sentiment
During: Oral Words
What's expressing
Primary: Written Words
Expressed opinions
Real Time
Offline
Legal SA & OM Polarity States
Sentiment Analysis (SA)
Sentiment Detected (SA SD1)
Sentiment Not Detected (SA SD0)
Opinion Mining (OM)
Opinion Detected (OM OD1)
Factual-Based (OM OD1-FB)
Non-Factual Based (OM OD1-NFB)
Opinion Not Detected (OM OD0)
Figure 4: Legal Sentiment Analysis & Opinion Mining – Four-Square Grid on Timing
Source Author: Dr. Lance B. Eliot
V1.3

Figure 17

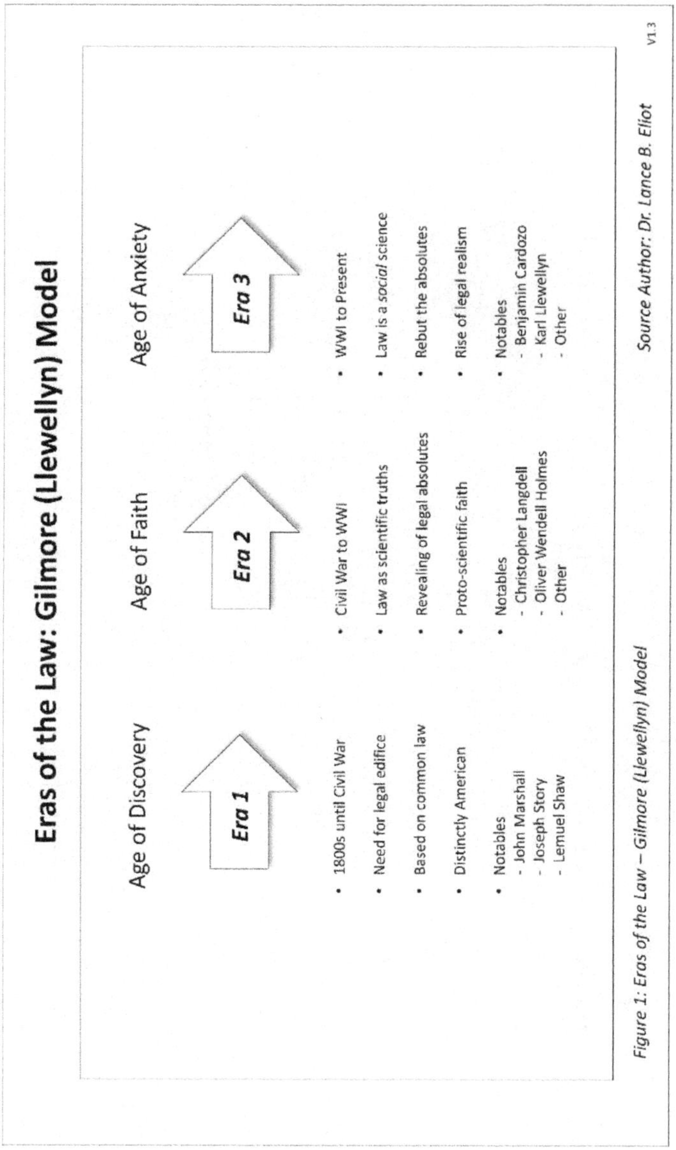
Eras of the Law: Gilmore (Llewellyn) Model
Age of Discovery
Era 1
• 1800s until Civil War
• Need for legal edifice
• Based on common law
• Distinctly American
• Notables
- John Marshall
- Joseph Story
- Lemuel Shaw
Age of Faith
Era 2
• Civil War to WWI
• Law as scientific truths
• Revealing of legal absolutes
• Proto-scientific faith
• Notables
- Christopher Langdell
- Oliver Wendell Holmes
- Other
Age of Anxiety
Era 3
• WWI to Present
• Law is a social science
• Rebut the absolutes
• Rise of legal realism
• Notables
- Benjamin Cardozo
- Karl Llewellyn
- Other
Figure 1: Eras of the Law – Gilmore (Llewellyn) Model
Source Author: Dr. Lance B. Eliot
V1.3

Figure 18

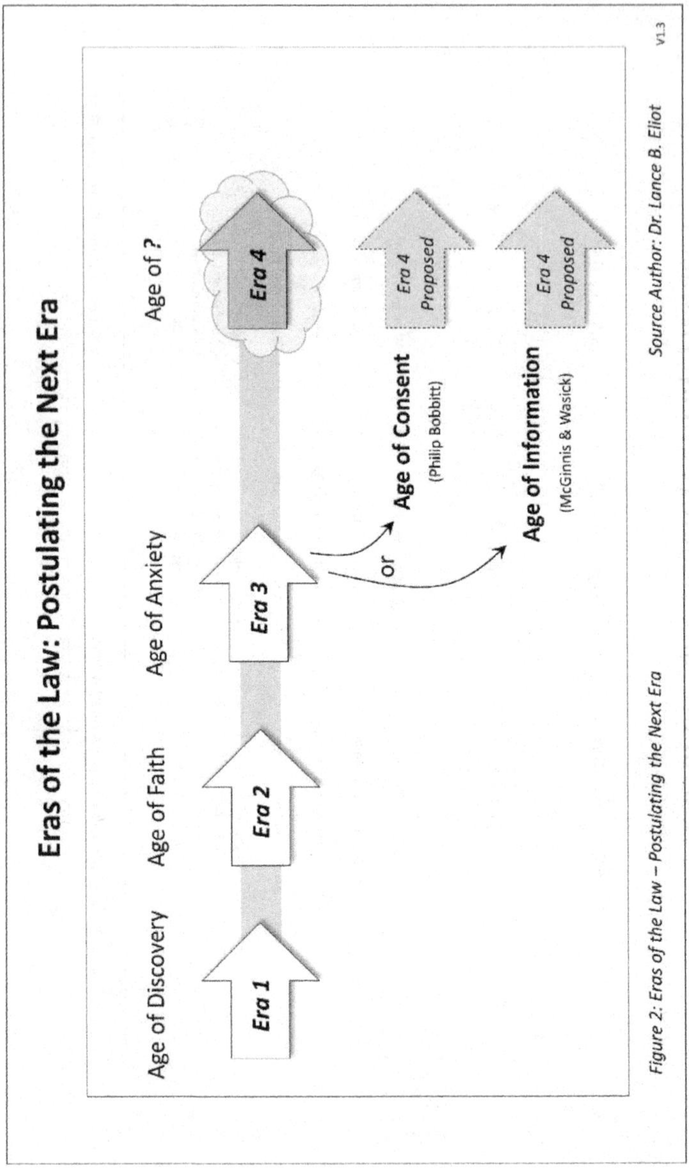
Eras of the Law: Postulating the Next Era
Age of Discovery
Age of Faith
Age of Anxiety
Age of ?
Era 1
Era 2
Era 3
Era 4
or
Age of Consent
(Philip Bobbitt)
Era 4
Proposed
Age of Information
(McGinnis & Wasick)
Era 4
Proposed
Figure 2: Eras of the Law – Postulating the Next Era
Source Author: Dr. Lance B. Eliot
V1.3

Figure 19

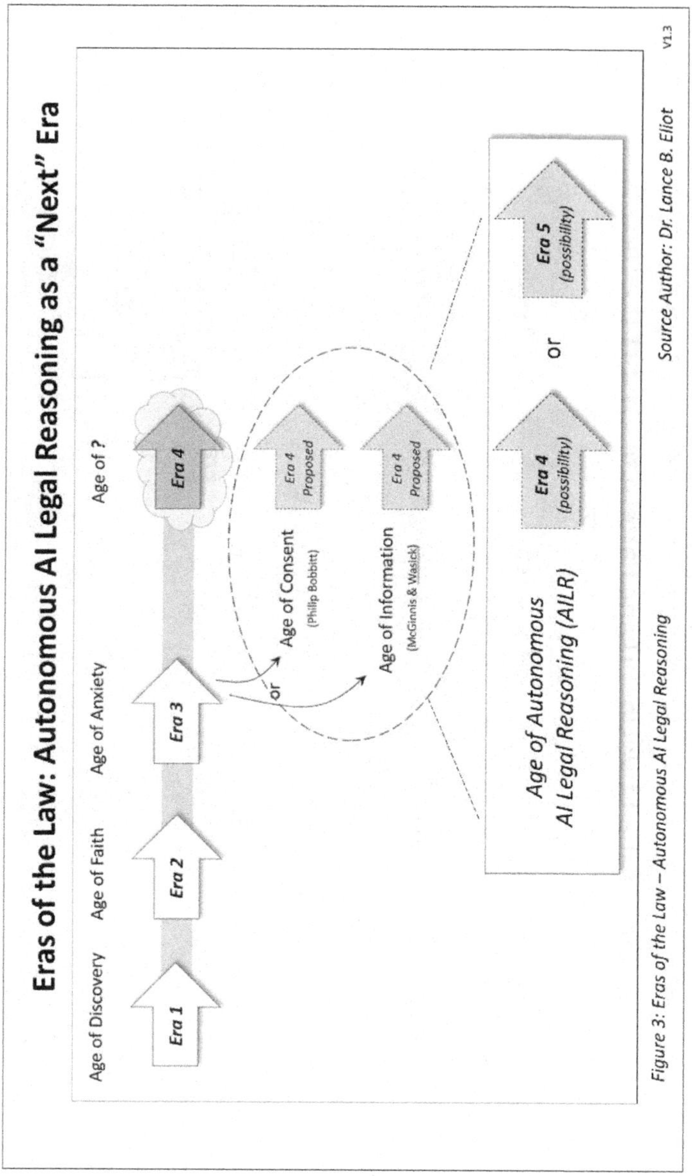
Eras of the Law: Autonomous AI Legal Reasoning as a "Next" Era
Age of Discovery
Age of Faith
Age of Anxiety
Age of ?
Era 1
Era 2
Era 3
Era 4
or
Age of Consent
(Philip Bobbitt)
Era 4 Proposed
Age of Information
(McGinnis & Wasick)
Era 4 Proposed
Age of Autonomous
AI Legal Reasoning (AILR)
Era 4
(possibility)
or
Era 5
(possibility)
Figure 3: Eras of the Law – Autonomous AI Legal Reasoning
Source Author: Dr. Lance B. Eliot
V1.3

Figure 20

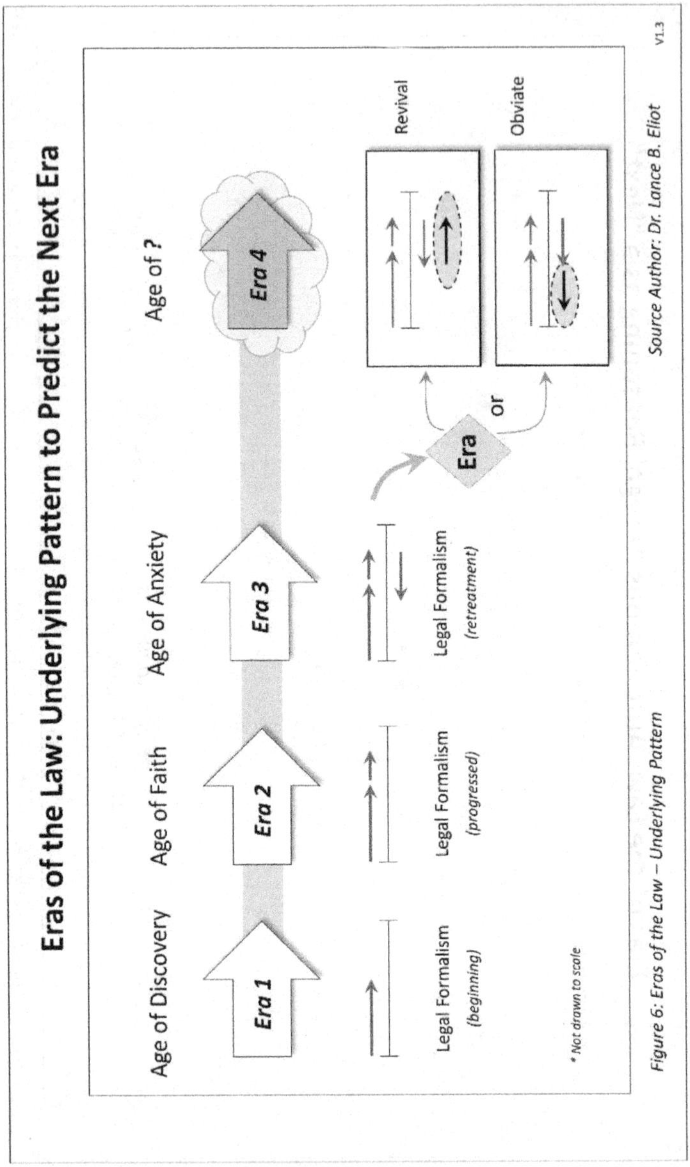
Eras of the Law: Underlying Pattern to Predict the Next Era
Age of Discovery
Age of Faith
Age of Anxiety
Age of ?
Era 1
Era 2
Era 3
Era 4
Legal Formalism
(beginning)
Legal Formalism
(progressed)
Legal Formalism
(retreatment)
Era
or
Revival
Obviate
* Not drawn to scale
Figure 6: Eras of the Law – Underlying Pattern
Source Author: Dr. Lance B. Eliot
V1.3

Figure 21

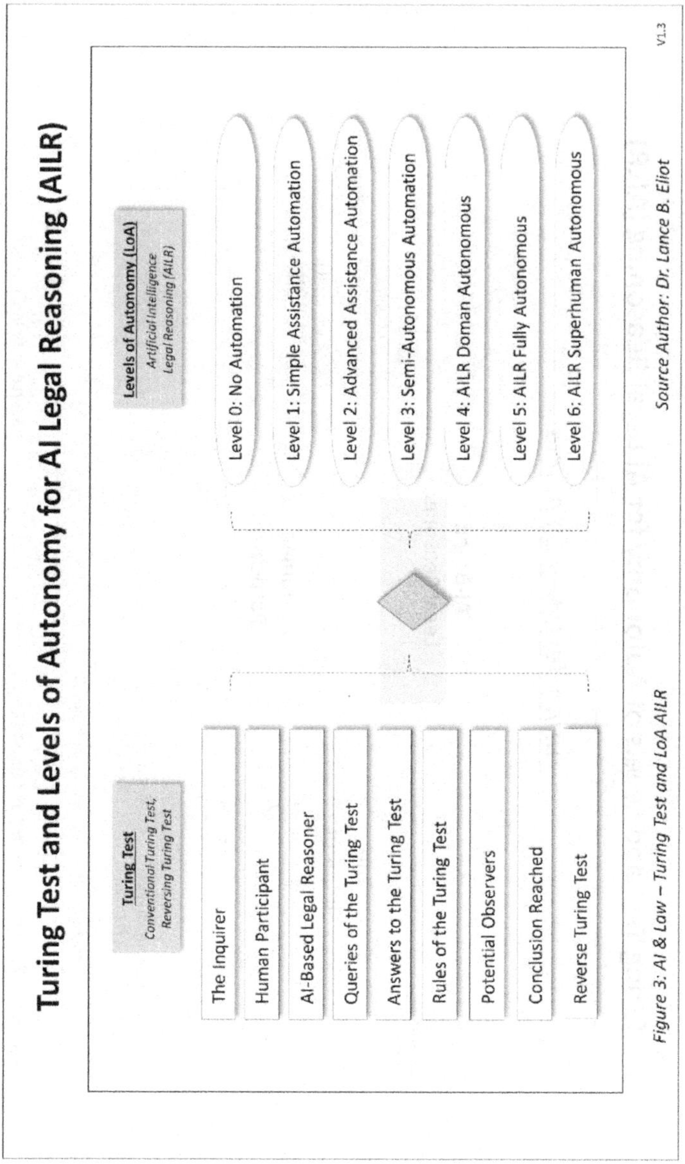
Turing Test and Levels of Autonomy for AI Legal Reasoning (AILR)
Turing Test
Conventional Turing Test, Reversing Turing Test
The Inquirer
Human Participant
AI-Based Legal Reasoner
Queries of the Turing Test
Answers to the Turing Test
Rules of the Turing Test
Potential Observers
Conclusion Reached
Reverse Turing Test
Levels of Autonomy (LoA)
Artificial Intelligence Legal Reasoning (AILR)
Level 0: No Automation
Level 1: Simple Assistance Automation
Level 2: Advanced Assistance Automation
Level 3: Semi-Autonomous Automation
Level 4: AILR Doman Autonomous
Level 5: AILR Fully Autonomous
Level 6: AILR Superhuman Autonomous
Figure 3: AI & Law – Turing Test and LoA AILR
Source Author: Dr. Lance B. Eliot
V1.3

Figure 22

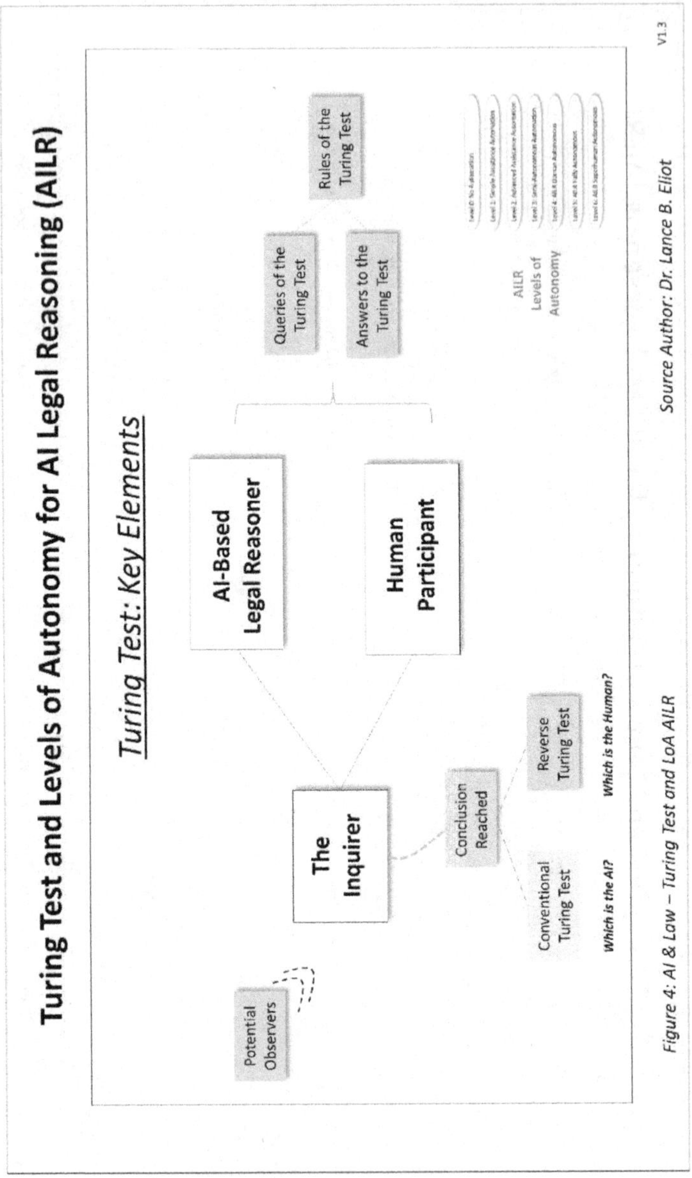
Turing Test and Levels of Autonomy for AI Legal Reasoning (AILR)
Turing Test: Key Elements
AI-Based Legal Reasoner
Human Participant
The Inquirer
Potential Observers
Queries of the Turing Test
Answers to the Turing Test
Rules of the Turing Test
AILR Levels of Autonomy
Conclusion Reached
Conventional Turing Test
Reverse Turing Test
Which is the AI?
Which is the Human?
Figure 4: AI & Law – Turing Test and LoA AILR
Source Author: Dr. Lance B. Eliot
V1.3

Figure 23

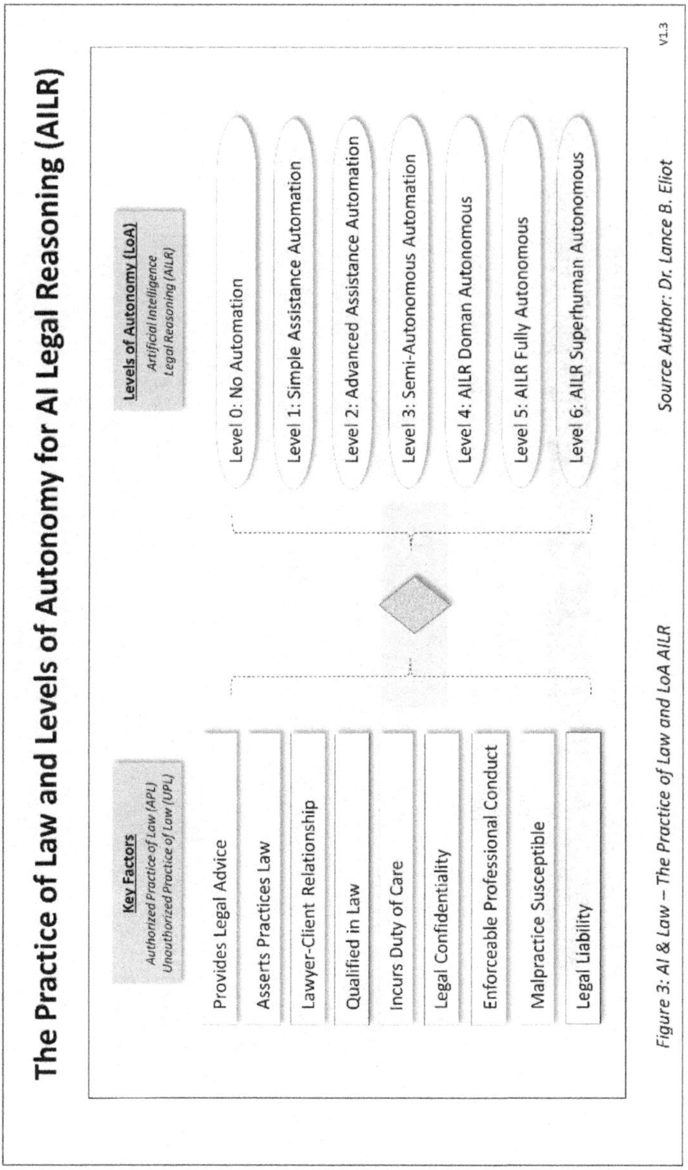
The Practice of Law and Levels of Autonomy for AI Legal Reasoning (AILR)
Key Factors
Authorized Practice of Law (APL)
Unauthorized Practice of Law (UPL)
Provides Legal Advice
Asserts Practices Law
Lawyer-Client Relationship
Qualified in Law
Incurs Duty of Care
Legal Confidentiality
Enforceable Professional Conduct
Malpractice Susceptible
Legal Liability
Levels of Autonomy (LoA)
Artificial Intelligence
Legal Reasoning (AILR)
Level 0: No Automation
Level 1: Simple Assistance Automation
Level 2: Advanced Assistance Automation
Level 3: Semi-Autonomous Automation
Level 4: AILR Doman Autonomous
Level 5: AILR Fully Autonomous
Level 6: AILR Superhuman Autonomous
Figure 3: AI & Law – The Practice of Law and LoA AILR
Source Author: Dr. Lance B. Eliot
V1.3

Figure 24

The Practice of Law and Autonomous Levels of AI Legal Reasoning (AILR)

Descriptor	Level 0 No Automation	Level 1 Simple Assistance Automation	Level 2 Advanced Assistance Automation	Level 3 Semi-Autonomous Automation	Level 4 AILR Domain Autonomous	Level 5 AILR Fully Autonomous	Level 6 AILR Superhuman Autonomous
Provides Legal Advice	n/a	No	Maybe	Yes	Yes	Yes	Yes Plus
Asserts Practices Law	n/a	No	No	No	Yes	Yes	Yes Plus
Lawyer-Client Relationship	n/a	No	No	No	Partial	Yes	Yes
Qualified in Law	n/a	No	No	Minimal	Partial	Yes	Yes Plus
Incurs Duty of Care	n/a	No	No	No	Likely	Yes	Yes
Legal Confidentiality	n/a	No	No	No	Likely	Yes	Yes
Enforceable Prof Conduct	n/a	No	No	No	Likely	Yes	Yes
Malpractice Susceptible	n/a	No	No	No	Likely	Yes	Yes
Legal Liability	n/a	No	Maybe	Likely	Likely	Yes	Yes

Figure 1: AI & Law – The Practice of Law and LoA AILR by Columns

Source Author: Dr. Lance B. Eliot

V1.3

Strawman Variant

Figure 25

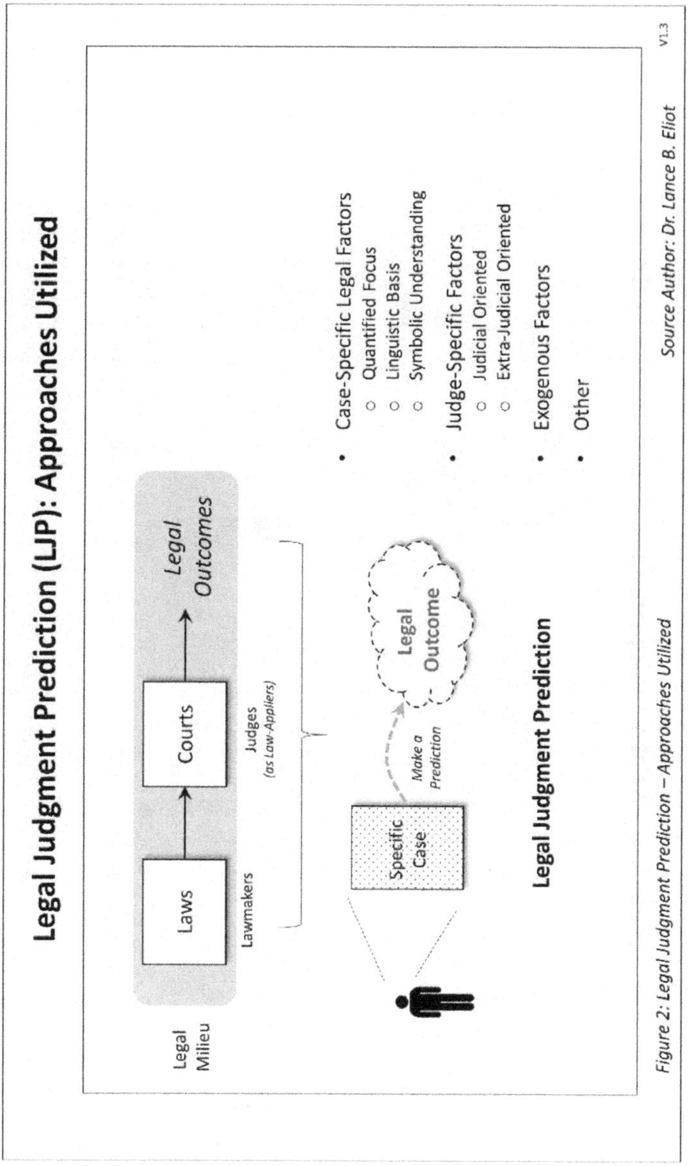

Legal Judgment Prediction (LJP): Approaches Utilized
Legal Milieu
Laws
Courts
Legal Outcomes
Lawmakers
Judges
(as Law-Appliers)
Specific Case
Make a Prediction
Legal Outcome
Legal Judgment Prediction
Case-Specific Legal Factors
Quantified Focus
Linguistic Basis
Symbolic Understanding
Judge-Specific Factors
Judicial Oriented
Extra-Judicial Oriented
Exogenous Factors
Other
Figure 2: Legal Judgment Prediction – Approaches Utilized
Source Author: Dr. Lance B. Eliot
V1.3

Figure 26

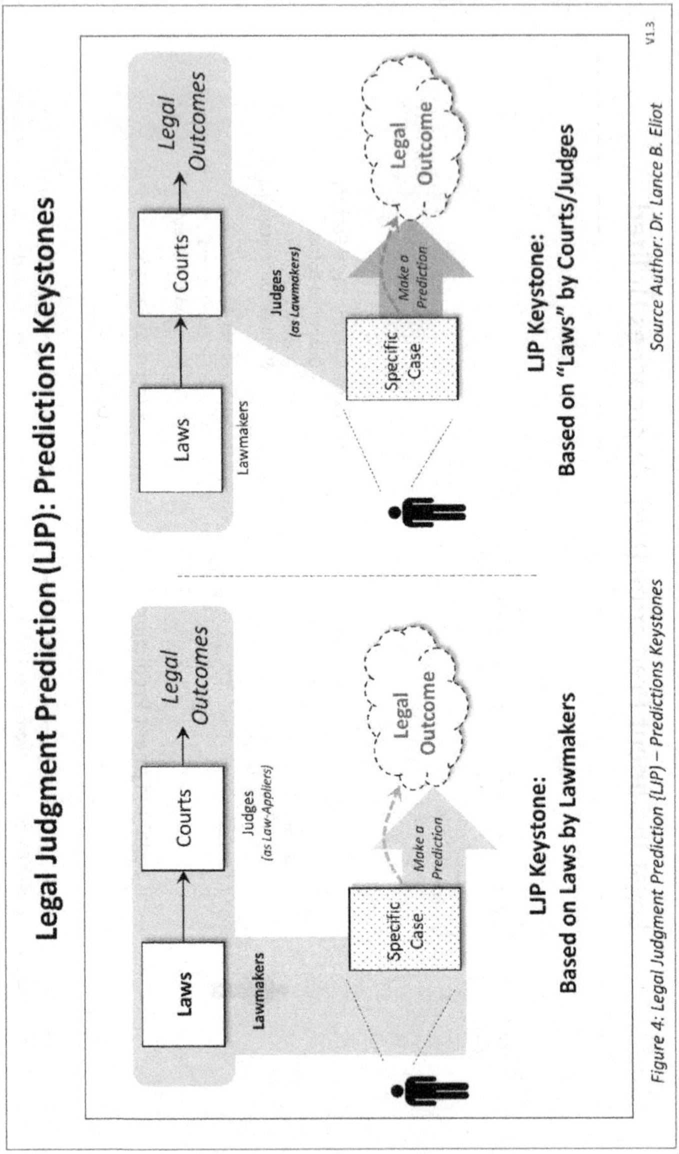
Legal Judgment Prediction (LJP): Predictions Keystones
Laws
Courts
Legal Outcomes
Lawmakers
Judges (as Law-Appliers)
Specific Case
Make a Prediction
Legal Outcome
LJP Keystone: Based on Laws by Lawmakers
Judges (as Lawmakers)
LJP Keystone: Based on "Laws" by Courts/Judges
Figure 4: Legal Judgment Prediction (LJP) – Predictions Keystones
Source Author: Dr. Lance B. Eliot
V1.3

Figure 27

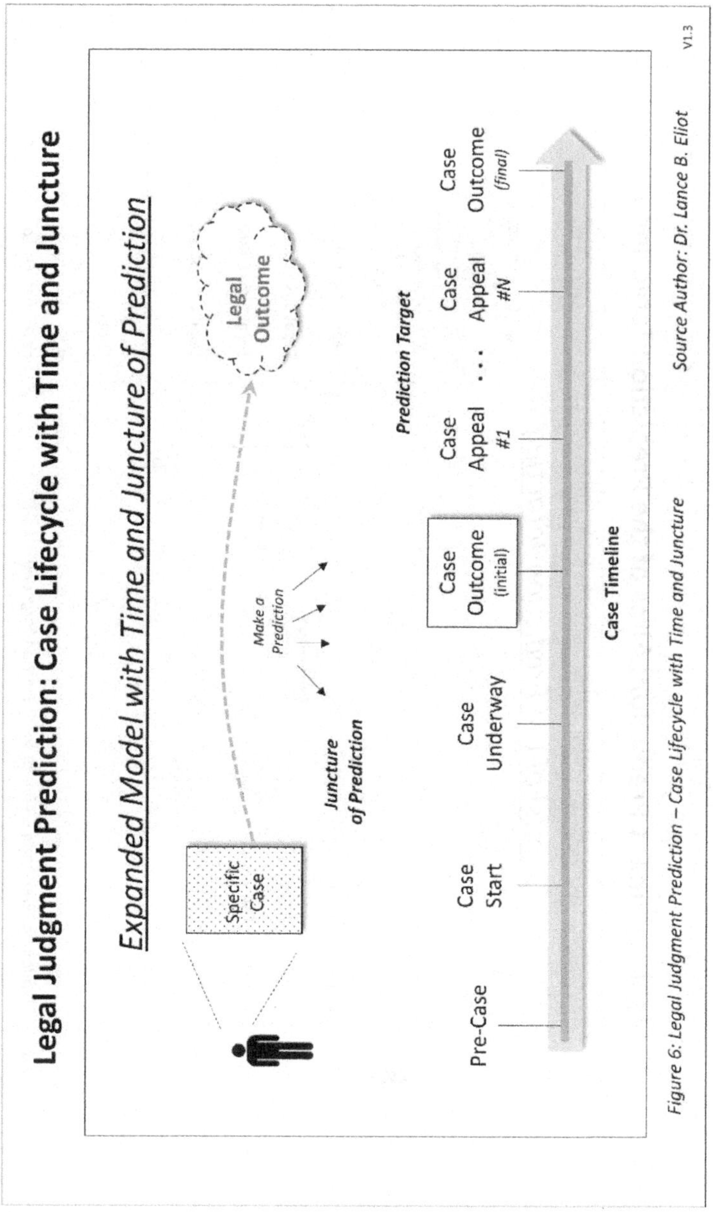
Legal Judgment Prediction: Case Lifecycle with Time and Juncture
Expanded Model with Time and Juncture of Prediction
Specific Case
Legal Outcome
Make a Prediction
Juncture of Prediction
Prediction Target
Pre-Case
Case Start
Case Underway
Case Outcome (initial)
Case Appeal #1
. . .
Case Appeal #N
Case Outcome (final)
Case Timeline
Figure 6: Legal Judgment Prediction – Case Lifecycle with Time and Juncture
Source Author: Dr. Lance B. Eliot
V1.3

Figure 28

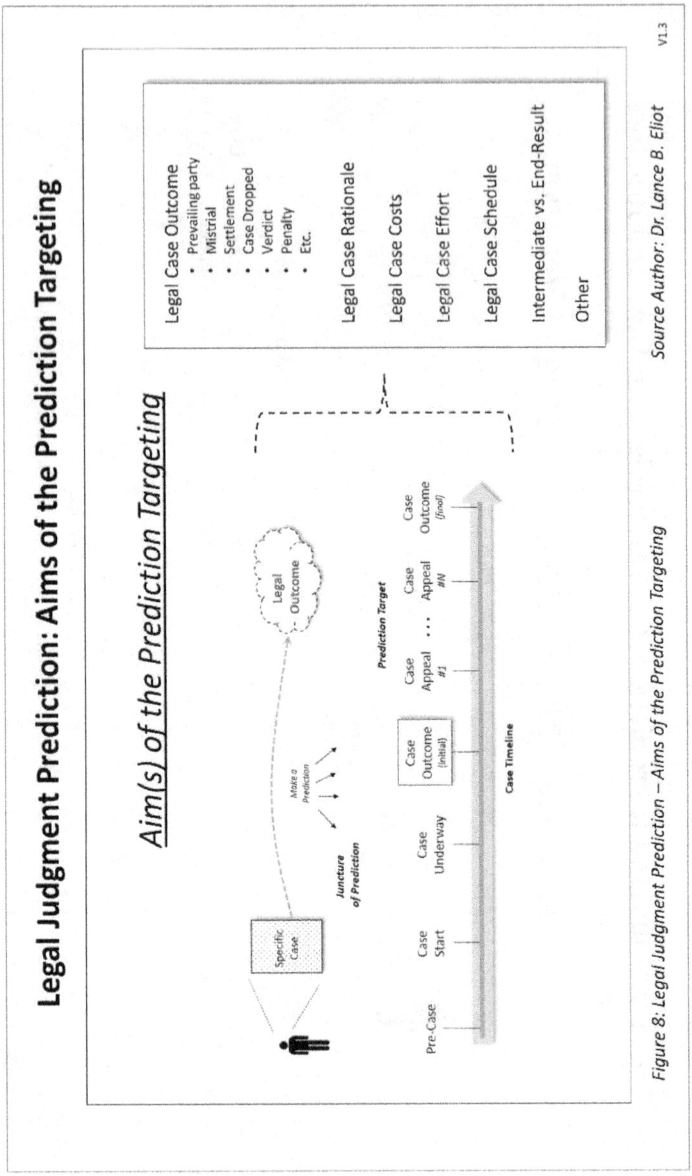
Legal Judgment Prediction: Aims of the Prediction Targeting
Aim(s) of the Prediction Targeting
Specific Case
Juncture of Prediction
Make a Prediction
Legal Outcome
Prediction Target
Pre-Case
Case Start
Case Underway
Case Outcome (initial)
Case Appeal #1
. . .
Case Appeal #N
Case Outcome (final)
Case Timeline
Legal Case Outcome
Prevailing party
Mistrial
Settlement
Case Dropped
Verdict
Penalty
Etc.
Legal Case Rationale
Legal Case Costs
Legal Case Effort
Legal Case Schedule
Intermediate vs. End-Result
Other
Figure 8: Legal Judgment Prediction – Aims of the Prediction Targeting
Source Author: Dr. Lance B. Eliot
V1.3

Figure 29

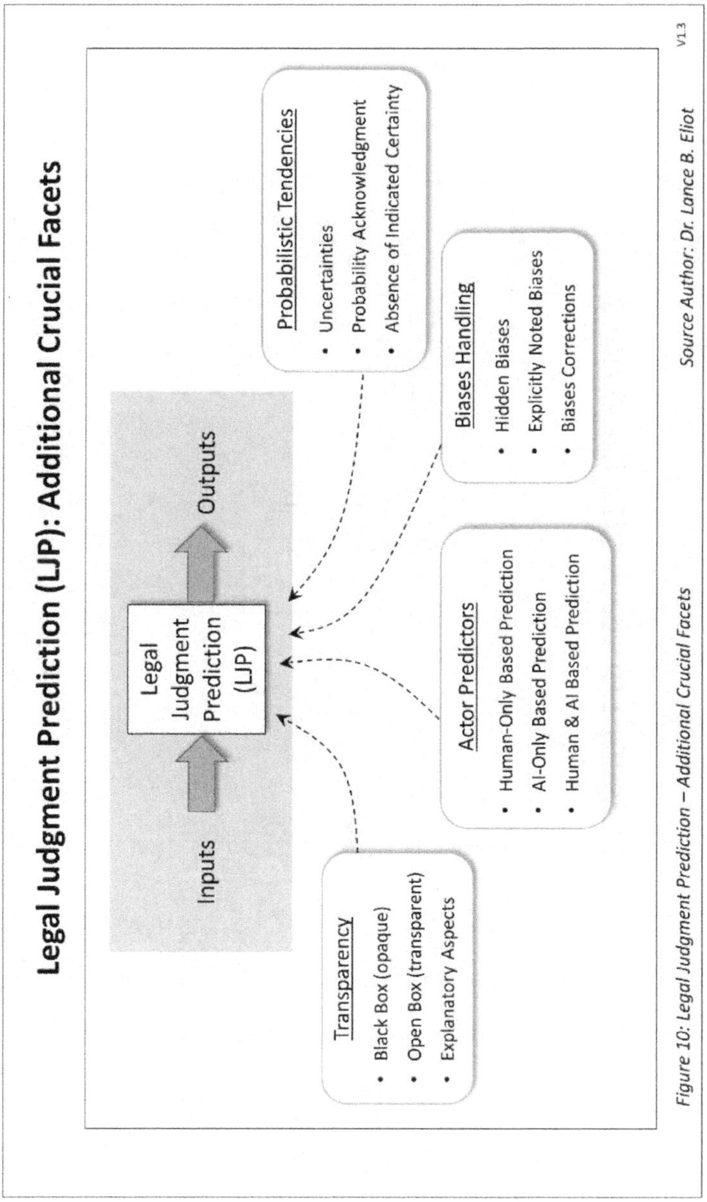

Figure 10: Legal Judgment Prediction – Additional Crucial Facets

Figure 30

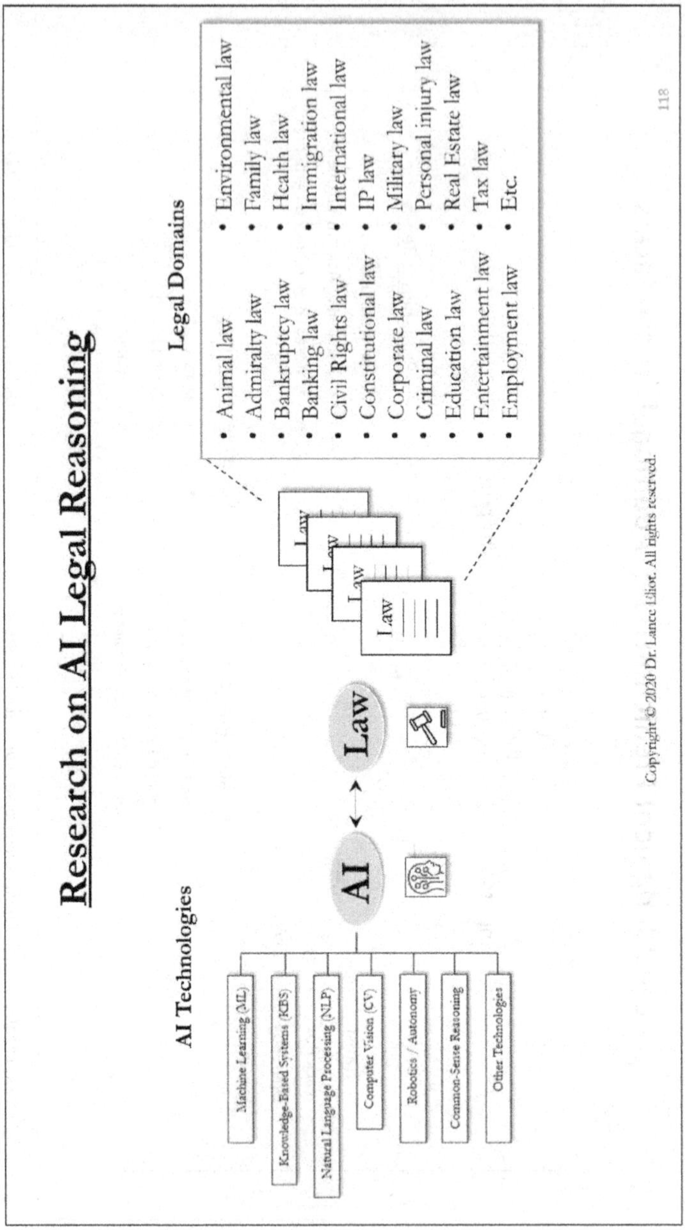
Research on AI Legal Reasoning
AI Technologies
Machine Learning (ML)
Knowledge-Based Systems (KBS)
Natural Language Processing (NLP)
Computer Vision (CV)
Robotics / Autonomy
Common-Sense Reasoning
Other Technologies
AI
Law
Law
Legal Domains
• Animal law
• Admiralty law
• Bankruptcy law
• Banking law
• Civil Rights law
• Constitutional law
• Corporate law
• Criminal law
• Education law
• Entertainment law
• Employment law
• Environmental law
• Family law
• Health law
• Immigration law
• International law
• IP law
• Military law
• Personal injury law
• Real Estate law
• Tax law
• Etc.
Copyright © 2020 Dr. Lance Eliot. All rights reserved.
118

Figure 31

Companion Book By Dr. Lance Eliot

"Artificial Intelligence and Legal Reasoning Essentials"

ISBN 978-1-73460165-7

Chapters

Available on Amazon and via other online book sellers

Companion Book By Dr. Lance Eliot

"Artificial Intelligence and LegalTech Essentials"

ISBN 978-1-7346016-3-3

Chapters

Available on Amazon and via other online book sellers

<u>Companion Book By Dr. Lance Eliot</u>

"Decisive Essays On AI And Law"

ISBN 978-1-73630310-8

Chapters

Available on Amazon and via other online book sellers

Companion Book By Dr. Lance Eliot

"Incisive Research On AI And Law"

ISBN 978-1-73630311-5

Chapters

Available on Amazon and via other online book sellers

Companion Book By Dr. Lance Eliot

"Ingenious Essays On AI And Law"

ISBN 978-1-73630312-2

Chapters

Available on Amazon and via other online book seller

Companion Book By Dr. Lance Eliot

"Compelling Essays On AI And Law"

ISBN 978-1-73630313-9

Chapters

Available on Amazon and via other online book sellers

Companion Book By Dr. Lance Eliot

"Topnotch Essays On AI And Law"

ISBN 978-1-73630314-6

Chapters

Available on Amazon and via other online book sellers

Companion Book By Dr. Lance Eliot

"Trendsetting Essays On AI And Law"

ISBN 978-1-95-738601-0

Chapters

Available on Amazon and via other online book sellers

Companion Book By Dr. Lance Eliot

"Pioneering Essays On AI And Law"

ISBN 978-1-95-738602-7

Chapters

Available on Amazon and via other online book sellers

Companion Book By Dr. Lance Eliot

"Trailblazing Essays On AI And Law"

ISBN 978-1-95-738602-7

Chapters

Available on Amazon and via other online book sellers

Companion Book By Dr. Lance Eliot

"Leading Edge Essays On AI And Law"

ISBN 978-1-95-738604-1

Chapters

Available on Amazon and via other online book sellers

Companion Book By Dr. Lance Eliot

"Jurisprudent Essays On AI And Law"

ISBN 978-1-95-738604-1

Chapters

Available on Amazon and via other online book sellers

ABOUT THE AUTHOR

Dr. Lance B. Eliot, Ph.D., MBA is a globally recognized AI expert and thought leader, an invited Stanford Fellow at Stanford University, an experienced top executive and corporate leader, a successful entrepreneur, and a noted scholar on AI, including that his Forbes and AI Trends columns have amassed over 4 million views, his books on AI are ranked in the Top 10 of all-time AI books, his journal articles are widely cited, and he has developed and implemented numerous AI systems.

He currently serves as the Chief AI Scientist at Techbruim, Inc. and has over twenty years of industry experience including serving as a corporate officer in billion-dollar sized firms and was a partner in a major consulting firm. He is also a successful entrepreneur having founded, ran, and sold several high-tech related businesses.

Dr. Eliot previously hosted the popular radio show *Technotrends* that was also available on American Airlines flights via their in-flight audio program, he has made appearances on CNN, has been a frequent speaker at industry conferences, and his podcasts have been downloaded over 150,000 times.

A former professor at the University of Southern California (USC), he founded and led an innovative research lab on Artificial Intelligence. He also previously served on the faculty of the University of California Los Angeles (UCLA) and was a visiting professor at other major universities. He was elected to the International Board of the Society for Information Management (SIM), a prestigious association of over 3,000 high-tech executives worldwide.

He has performed extensive community service, including serving as Senior Science Adviser to the Congressional Vice-Chair of the Congressional Committee on Science & Technology. He has served on the Board of the OC Science & Engineering Fair (OCSEF), where he is also has been a Grand Sweepstakes judge, and likewise served as a judge for the Intel International SEF (ISEF). He served as the Vice-Chair of the Association for Computing Machinery (ACM) Chapter, a prestigious association of computer scientists. Dr. Eliot has been a shark tank judge for the USC Mark Stevens Center for Innovation on start-up pitch competitions and served as a mentor for several incubators and accelerators in Silicon Valley and in Silicon Beach.

Dr. Eliot holds a Ph.D. from USC, MBA, and Bachelor's in Computer Science, and earned the CDP, CCP, CSP, CDE, and CISA certification.

ADDENDUM

Thanks for reading this book and I hope you will continue your interest in the field of AI & Law

---

For my free podcasts about AI & Law:

https://ai-law.libsyn.com/website

Those podcasts are also available on Spotify, iTunes, etc.

For the latest on AI & Law see my website:

www.ai-law.legal

To follow me on Twitter:

https://twitter.com/LanceEliot

For my in-depth book on AI & Law:

AI And Legal Reasoning Essentials

www.amazon.com/gp/product/1734601655/

Made in the USA
Monee, IL
05 November 2026

67808617R00134